"All Scripture is inspired by God and is useful for teaching the truth, rebuking error, correcting faults, and giving instructions for right living, so that the person who serves God may be fully qualified and equipped to do every kind of good deed."

2 Timothy 3:16-17
Good News Bible

Sunday Gospel Readings with *Lectio Divina*

Year A: Year of Matthew

Our springboard into the year of Matthew, year A of the three-year lectionary cycle, has been two remarkable events which took place in 2010. The Edinburgh 2010 Conference in June, marking the centenary of the 1910 World Missionary Conference and the visit in September of Pope Benedict XVI.

Like Matthew's Gospel, the two events remind us that the revelation of God's love in Jesus Christ is fundamentally incarnational – rooted in humanity and in the unfolding of human history.

Once again we commend to you this prayerful resource, which invites us, through the ancient Christian practice of Lectio Divina, to allow the Word of God to take root in our heart and give direction to our life, so that in all we are and do and say, we will bear witness that Jesus Christ is truly the Son of God; that his word is ever ancient and ever new; and his command to bring the Gospel to the ends of the earth is as urgent today as it has ever been.

Catholic Bishops' Conference of Scotland

SCOTTISH
BIBLE SOCIETY
The Word for the world

These *Lectio Divina* outlines are also available in Albanian, Dutch, French, Greek, Maltese, Portuguese, Slovak, Slovenian, Spanish and other languages. For full details visit **www.wordforliving.org**

Acknowledgement: Thanks to the American Bible Society www.americanbible.org for granting permission to adapt material from *Encuentro Con La Biblia/Encounter With the Bible* for use in the introduction.

For enquiries: info@ubs-europe.org

INTRODUCTION

These weekly outlines combine the Liturgy's Sunday Gospel readings with the *lectio divina* approach to Holy Scripture.

Lectio divina is a dynamic, life-oriented approach to reading Holy Scriptures encouraged by both Pope John Paul II and Pope Benedict XVI. It provides a framework for a faithful and respectful reading of the Bible that is sincere and authentic.

Lectio divina is a blessing for the entire Church as it opens up the rich truths of Scripture for every Christian. Through it believers are invited to read, understand and deepen their appreciation of the Scriptures and to seek guidance for their lives in the teaching of the Lord Jesus.

Our real goal is to meet our Lord as we read his Word and allow him to transform our lives to be more like him through the work of the Holy Spirit.

All the information necessary for you to have a meaningful encounter with God's Word is included in this booklet. These outlines can be used individually or in groups.

The following pages introduce the four steps of *lectio divina* with some extra tips for using these outlines in groups.

ABOUT LECTIO DIVINA

History

Lectio divina dates back to the early Church Fathers around 300 AD. The four steps were first recorded by a monk, Guigo Cartujo, in 1173. These steps Lectio (Reading), Meditatio (Meditation), Oratio (Prayer) and Contemplatio (Contemplation) remain central today although methods differ.

Overview

In essence *lectio divina* is a simple way to meet with the Lord through reflection and prayer based on Holy Scripture. It is not a study method. Background knowledge can be helpful but is not essential.

Used in groups a structure is necessary but for individuals the steps need not be followed rigidly. Our aim is meeting God, not just completing the steps themselves. So when the Lord impresses something on us we need to stop and wait. We can always come back to the steps another time. We don't want to lose what God is saying to us.

LECTIO – READING

Reading the Scripture passage humbly and prayerfully is the foundation for everything else that follows and cannot be rushed. So begin with a prayer and ask the Holy Spirit to 'lead you into all the truth' (John 16:13).

Read the passage slowly and carefully. Avoid being tempted to look at the Lectio comments or any of the other steps at this stage.

Have a notebook and pencil ready. Underline, or make a note of, any words or phrases that stand out to you. Write down any questions that occur to you. Read the passage several times and read it aloud. Give yourself time to understand and appreciate what is being said.

Now read the Lectio comments and reflect on the ways they are similar or different to your first thoughts.

 MEDITATIO – MEDITATION

Meditation deepens our appreciation of the passage and helps us to explore its riches. We read in 2 Timothy 3:16 that 'All Scripture is inspired by God and is useful for teaching the truth, rebuking error, correcting faults, and giving instructions for right living...' So approach Scripture in faith expecting God to speak to you. He may reveal something of himself to you. He might highlight an attitude or behaviour of yours that needs to change. He might show you a promise to encourage and strengthen you.

Here are some suggested approaches you may find helpful.

Use your imagination. Picture the passage; put yourself into the scene and become part of the story. See things through the eyes of the other characters, listen to what they say, watch their reactions, imagine how they feel. Keep coming back to Jesus. Get to know him; delight yourself and become fascinated by him, his words, his actions, the way he responds – everything about him.

Ask questions. Use your own questions and the questions given to think more deeply about the passage and what God wants to say to you. Ask Jesus why he did and said what he did. Try to understand his reasons and intentions. Allow time to be quiet, to listen and hear his answer.

Let the Word be a mirror for you. As we read the Bible it shows us more of what the Christian life looks like and where ours needs to change. We see how God's Word applies to our daily life, as an individual, and as part of our community and society. We will find promises and encouragement, challenges and demands. If we are willing God will nurture and free us to be more fully human and fully alive.

ORATIO – PRAYER

Prayer opens up a conversation between God and us. In the Psalms we see how the writers pour out their feelings to God, often mixing hopes and fears side by side. God values our honesty. We can't hide anything from him anyway. Using the words of the responsorial psalm can help us but we can also use our own words to have a heart-to-heart conversation with a very special friend.

Through prayer we make our response to the light God's Word has shed on how we are living our lives. Now we can bring what is happening in our own life and in our community before God. We speak and listen, listen and reflect – it is a conversation with God.

 CONTEMPLATIO – CONTEMPLATION

To help us interpret the Gospel reading the Liturgy provides two further Scripture readings. Reflecting on these can both enrich our understanding of the text and bring into focus a response we may need to make to the Lord.

Contemplation gives us the opportunity for an intimate time of communion with God. Be still before God and invite him in. Few words, if any, are necessary here. Enjoy time in his presence. Just be with him and let him love you. Let him refresh your soul.

Review

After you have finished your time of reading, meditation, prayer and contemplation you may want to jot down in a notebook any experiences or thoughts that particularly impressed you. You may find it helpful to look back at these later.

USING THESE OUTLINES IN GROUPS

When *lectio divina* is used in a group a little preparation is needed.

 LECTIO:

Try one or more of the following ways of reading the passage. See what works best for your particular group.

Individual reading. To start with give everyone time to read through the passage silently.

Proclamation of the Word. One person reads (proclaims) the Word. This is the traditional manner of reading in the liturgical celebration.

Two readers. Two people read the text aloud alternately.

Each person reads a verse. This is a way of involving each participant, inviting each to read from his own Bible, so that the reading is attentive and dynamic.

Audio version. If you have access to a recorded version of the text you could also use that. You may notice different words are stressed.

With different characters. Approach the text somewhat like a drama, in which one person is the narrator/reader, another takes the part of Jesus, a third takes another character. This can be the most dynamic or engaging method and helps us to identify just what the different characters in the passage are saying.

 MEDITATIO:

- In the group setting, it is important that everyone is given time to participate, to share what the Lord has been saying to them. While the Lord speaks through his Word, he also speaks to us through our brothers and sisters. So as we listen to others we need to open our hearts to hear the Lord's voice speaking through them.

- It is important that everyone in the group understands that this sharing is to build one another up and enrich our experience. It is not necessary that everyone agrees about what is shared. You need to be careful to avoid this time turning into a debate or argument. The Lord knows us each as individuals so will have different things to say to us personally at this specific point in our lives.

- You can start with a simple question like "What catches your attention in this passage?" and use the printed questions. The aim is to help everyone feel comfortable to speak and share how the text has inspired them. Gently keep the group focused on the text and what God is saying.

ORATIO:

We suggest you give people time for personal silent prayer before God. You can also give opportunity for people to pray out loud in their own words and use verses from the responsorial prayer. The aim should be to help each person make a personal response to the Lord during this time.

 CONTEMPLATIO:

Contemplation by its very nature is an individual exercise and silence is necessary. If you have room it may be helpful to suggest people move so they have their own 'personal space'.

*The Scripture references for the Psalms follow the Hebrew numbering used in many recent Bibles including the Jerusalem Bible but some Bibles use different numbering. If Psalm 23 The Good Shepherd is numbered as Psalm 22 in your Bible, please refer to your church lectionary for all the correct Psalm references for your Bible.

BE PREPARED

Matthew 24:37-44

[37] The coming of the Son of Man will be like what happened in the time of Noah. [38] In the days before the flood people ate and drank, men and women married, up to the very day Noah went into the boat; [39] yet they did not realize what was happening until the flood came and swept them all away. That is how it will be when the Son of Man comes. [40] At that time two men will be working in a field: one will be taken away, the other will be left behind. [41] Two women will be at a mill grinding meal: one will be taken away, the other will be left behind.

[42] "Be on your guard, then, because you do not know what day your Lord will come. [43] If the owner of a house knew the time when the thief would come, you can be sure that he would stay awake and not let the thief break into his house. [44] So then, you also must always be ready, because the Son of Man will come at an hour when you are not expecting him.

*Other Readings: Isaiah 2:1-5; *Psalm 122:1-2, 4-9; Romans 13:11-14*

 LECTIO:

The first Sunday of Advent marks not only the preparation for Christmas and the birth of Jesus but also the beginning of the liturgical year. And the Church chooses to open the year with a big wake-up call: be ready, don't let the world distract you from your real purpose.

Matthew – our Gospel writer for the better part of the coming year – portrays end-time events using graphic language and striking images.

Apocalyptic teaching, as this is known, is usually given in harsh times when people are suffering. The three synoptic Gospel writers Matthew, Mark and Luke each give this type of teaching. We can also read it in much greater depth in the challenging book of prophecy for the end times, the book of Revelation.

In today's reading Jesus preaches and gives a warning he has given several times as he prepares to return to Jerusalem for his Passion. He again uses powerful images to highlight the unexpected nature of the end times.

He uses three different images to paint the picture of how suddenly the end will come. It will come at a time when people are not expecting it, without any warning, like a flood sweeping all but a few away.

See note at the end of the Introduction on the previous page.

But here Jesus also tells us of the gathering together of the faithful by the 'Son of Man', a title first used in the Old Testament book of Daniel and adopted by Jesus, the Messiah.

 MEDITATIO:

- How do you react to Jesus' teaching that he might return at any time?
- Consider the phrase 'they didn't realise what was happening'. Why not? Does this apply to people today? How might we respond to this?
- Think about the comparison to the flood that came in Noah's day. What can we learn from this?
- God makes the final choice to take one person and not another – even if outwardly they appear the same. What differences might there be?
- What can we learn from Paul's teaching in Romans 13:11-14?

 ORATIO:

Prayerfully consider your relationship with the Lord. How ready are you for Jesus' return? Ask the Lord to show you any changes you might need to make.

Pray for the Lord to reveal himself to those who do not know him yet.

 CONTEMPLATIO:

Read the prophecy in Isaiah 2:1-5. Spend some time reflecting on these phrases:

'He will teach us what he wants us to do; we will walk in the paths he has chosen.'

'...let us walk in the light which the Lord gives us!'

Consider too these words from 1 Thessalonians 5:23-24:

'May the God who gives us peace make you holy in every way and keep your whole being – spirit, soul, and body – free from every fault at the coming of our Lord Jesus Christ. He who calls you will do it, because he is faithful.'

COME TO JESUS

Matthew 3:1-12

¹ At that time John the Baptist came to the desert of Judea and started preaching. ² "Turn away from your sins," he said, "because the Kingdom of heaven is near!" ³ John was the man the prophet Isaiah was talking about when he said:

"Someone is shouting in the desert,
'Prepare a road for the Lord;
make a straight path for him to travel!' "

⁴ John's clothes were made of camel's hair; he wore a leather belt round his waist, and his food was locusts and wild honey. ⁵ People came to him from Jerusalem, from the whole province of Judea, and from all the country near the River Jordan. ⁶ They confessed their sins, and he baptized them in the Jordan.

⁷ When John saw many Pharisees and Sadducees coming to him to be baptized, he said to them, "You snakes – who told you that you could escape from the punishment God is about to send? ⁸ Do those things that will show that you have turned from your sins. ⁹ And don't think you can escape punishment by saying that Abraham is your ancestor. I tell you that God can take these stones and make descendants for Abraham! ¹⁰ The axe is ready to cut down the trees at the roots; every tree that does not bear good fruit will be cut down and thrown in the fire. ¹¹ I baptize you with water to show that you have repented, but the one who will come after me will baptize you with the Holy Spirit and fire. He is much greater than I am; and I am not good enough even to carry his sandals. ¹² He has his winnowing shovel with him to thresh out all the grain. He will gather his wheat into his barn, but he will burn the chaff in a fire that never goes out."

Other Readings: Isaiah 11:1-10; Psalm 72:1-2, 7-8, 12-13, 17; Romans 15:4-9

 LECTIO:

The whole purpose of Advent is laid out before us in the second verse of today's Gospel reading: turn away from your sins because the Kingdom of heaven (Matthew's usual expression for the Kingdom of God) is near. John's message repeats Jesus' warning in last week's Gospel message: make sure you are ready for the return of the King.

Matthew uses four powerful images – a road, water, an axe and fire – to remind us that while God's kingdom offers salvation and deliverance it also brings judgement and division.

This is where Matthew introduces John the Baptist to his readers and he emphasizes his significance straight away. Firstly, he identifies him as the person sent to prepare the way for the long awaited Messiah (Isaiah 40:3). Next, by describing John's clothing, he draws a comparison with one of Israel's greatest prophets, Elijah (2 Kings 1:8). The significance of baptising people in the river Jordan would not have been missed either; a thousand years earlier Joshua had miraculously led their ancestors through the Jordan to inherit the promised land.

John's message touched a nerve. People came in droves and repented. John's stern rebuke for the Pharisees and Sadducees makes it clear that he wasn't interested in an outward show of repentance. God is looking for genuine repentance that leads to changed lives – only this is worthy of the King. Relying on their spiritual pedigree as the sons of Abraham wasn't good enough.

And John was clear, right from the outset, about where his ministry ended and the Messiah took over.

 MEDITATIO:

- How would you explain the difference between the ministries of John and Jesus?
- What aspects of your life does God's grace cover?
- What is the 'good fruit' that we should expect to see in our lives as Christians?

 ORATIO:

John called for repentance and a turning towards God. What is God saying to you now?

 CONTEMPLATIO:

John was preparing the way for Jesus and pointing people towards him. We are called to do this as well – Jesus has made us fishers of men. What practical steps can you take during Advent to prepare yourself and others for the Messiah's rule?

FAITH IN JESUS

Matthew 11:2-11

² When John the Baptist heard in prison about the things that Christ was doing, he sent some of his disciples to him. ³ "Tell us," they asked Jesus, "are you the one John said was going to come, or should we expect someone else?"

⁴ Jesus answered, "Go back and tell John what you are hearing and seeing: ⁵ the blind can see, the lame can walk, those who suffer from dreaded skin diseases are made clean, the deaf hear, the dead are brought back to life, and the Good News is preached to the poor. ⁶ How happy are those who have no doubts about me!"

⁷ While John's disciples were leaving, Jesus spoke about him to the crowds: "When you went out to John in the desert, what did you expect to see? A blade of grass bending in the wind? ⁸ What did you go out to see? A man dressed up in fancy clothes? People who dress like that live in palaces! ⁹ Tell me, what did you go out to see? A prophet? Yes indeed, but you saw much more than a prophet. ¹⁰ For John is the one of whom the scripture says: 'God said, I will send my messenger ahead of you to open the way for you.' ¹¹ I assure you that John the Baptist is greater than anyone who has ever lived. But the one who is least in the Kingdom of heaven is greater than John.

Other Readings: Isaiah 35:1-6, 10; Psalm 146:6-10; James 5:7-10

 LECTIO:

Today's reading focuses on John the Baptist again, not this time in his role preparing the way for the Messiah but rather as a witness to Jesus' Messianic ministry.

John the Baptist is in prison but has been told about what Jesus is doing. He is puzzled. Jesus' actions don't seem to match up with the axe, fire and judgement John had told people the Messiah would bring (see last week's reading in Matthew 3:7-12). Had he made a mistake? Was someone else 'the one who is to come'? So he sends some of his disciples to ask Jesus directly.

Jesus doesn't give a direct answer but tells John's disciples to report the evidence – people are healed, the dead raised to life and the Good News is preached to the poor. He wants John to understand that he is indeed the Messiah and is bringing in the Kingdom of heaven as foretold by Old Testament prophets like Isaiah (see Isaiah 35:5-6, 61:1).

We are not told John's response but Jesus commends his integrity and confirms that John is indeed the 'messenger' sent to prepare the way for the Messiah as prophesied by Malachi (3:1).

John's prophetic role was to denounce sin and call for repentance. The message was the same for everyone – kings, religious leaders, ordinary people – and he was not afraid to speak out. It got him thrown into prison for condemning King Herod's marriage to his brother's wife and ultimately cost him his life (Matthew 14:3-12).

 ## MEDITATIO:

- Jesus wants us to grasp who he is for ourselves. Write down who you think Jesus is. You may want to add to this from time to time as Jesus reveals more of himself to you.
- Why do you think people who have no doubts about Jesus are 'happy' (v6)?
- How did John respond when he did not understand what Jesus was doing? What can we learn from this and the answer Jesus gave him?
- John was no blade of grass blowing in the wind. How does the cold wind of criticism or mockery affect you? Can you stand up for your faith?

 ## ORATIO:

God continues to intervene in history and individual lives to bring healing, help and peace. Read Psalm 146 to remind yourself of God's goodness and faithfulness. Use this to offer him your thanks and praise.

Wait before God in prayer. He may prompt you to pray for specific people who need his help and intervention in their lives right now.

 ## CONTEMPLATIO:

Time after time in scripture we read accounts of how God intervenes in people's lives bringing forgiveness, healing and guidance. Spend some time reflecting on the ways God has intervened in your life.

ANGELIC INTERVENTION

Matthew 1:18-24

[18] This was how the birth of Jesus Christ took place. His mother Mary was engaged to Joseph, but before they were married, she found out that she was going to have a baby by the Holy Spirit. [19] Joseph was a man who always did what was right, but he did not want to disgrace Mary publicly; so he made plans to break the engagement privately. [20] While he was thinking about this, an angel of the Lord appeared to him in a dream and said, "Joseph, descendant of David, do not be afraid to take Mary to be your wife. For it is by the Holy Spirit that she has conceived. [21] She will have a son, and you will name him Jesus – because he will save his people from their sins."

[22] Now all this happened in order to make what the Lord had said through the prophet come true, [23] "A virgin will become pregnant and have a son, and he will be called Immanuel" (which means, "God is with us").

[24] So when Joseph woke up, he married Mary, as the angel of the Lord had told him to do.

Other Readings: Isaiah 7:10-14; Psalm 24:1-6, 7, 10; Romans 1:1-7

 LECTIO:

We are now in the days leading up to Jesus' birth. In the preceding verses, Matthew has set out Jesus' lineage through King David, right back to Abraham, the father of the Jewish nation. God promised Abraham that through his descendants God would bless the whole human race (Genesis 12:2-3).

We are familiar with Mary's encounter with the angel Gabriel as told in Luke 1:26-38 but Matthew just chooses to say that 'she found out she was going to have a baby by the Holy Spirit'.

Matthew focuses instead on Joseph's angelic encounter. Joseph is engaged to be married but his fiancée Mary has told him she is pregnant. He knows he is not the father and so is planning to break off the engagement. At that time in Jewish society an engagement was legally binding; it could only be broken by a formal act of divorce.

Joseph clearly cares for Mary and wants to end the engagement privately to minimise the disgrace to her. While he is thinking about this an angel appears to him in a dream and tells him not to be afraid to marry Mary. The angel confirms to Joseph what Gabriel had told Mary – that the baby was conceived by the Holy Spirit, would be a son and they should name him Jesus.

Jesus was a popular boy's name at the time, which in Hebrew means 'the Lord saves'. It reminded people of their great ancestor Joshua (whose name had the same meaning) who led the Israelites out of exile in the wilderness and into the promised land after the death of Moses. But, the angel adds, this 'Joshua' will save people in a very specific way, not from physical exile but from 'their sins'.

Matthew interprets these events as a direct fulfilment of God's promise in Isaiah 7:14 to send Immanuel, 'God is with us'. So this baby not only has an ordinary everyday name but another very special name given to no one else.

Joseph, like Mary in the Gospel of Luke, believes and acts on what the angel tells him and they get married. After the birth of their baby, it is Joseph that names him Jesus. In doing so he identifies himself as Jesus' legal 'father' and, as a descendant of King David, he gives him royal lineage.

Joseph faithfully plays his part along with Mary in God's salvation plan. He helps provide a home for Jesus to grow up in before he fulfils his mission on earth.

MEDITATIO:

- Think about Joseph. How must he have felt when Mary told him an angel had told her she would be the mother of God's son? Or that she was pregnant by the power of the Holy Spirit?
- What lessons can you draw from Joseph's willingness to act quickly when he knew what God wanted him to do?
- Jesus came to save people from their sins. What does this mean for you?
- God gives grace and strength to cope in impossible situations. Where and when has he helped you?

ORATIO:

Read over today's verses from Psalm 24 several times. Use them to bring your praise to the great king.

CONTEMPLATIO:

God promised to send a Messiah to save his people. Think about his faithfulness. Marvel that Jesus came to earth as Immanuel, 'God is with us'. What does this mean for you?

A PROMISE FULFILLED

Luke 2:15-20

[15] When the angels went away from them back into heaven, the shepherds said to one another, "Let's go to Bethlehem and see this thing that has happened, which the Lord has told us."

[16] So they hurried off and found Mary and Joseph and saw the baby lying in the manger. [17] When the shepherds saw him, they told them what the angel had said about the child. [18] All who heard it were amazed at what the shepherds said. [19] Mary remembered all these things and thought deeply about them. [20] The shepherds went back, singing praises to God for all they had heard and seen; it had been just as the angel had told them.

Other Readings: Isaiah 62:11-12, Psalm 97:1, 6, 11-12; Titus 3:4-7

 LECTIO:

Today we celebrate our Saviour's birth and remind ourselves of another angelic visitation, this time to shepherds. To get the full story take a look at the first 14 verses of Luke 2.

What an amazing encounter this is. The shepherds on that lonely hillside must have been shocked to the core of their being when suddenly an angel appears and speaks to them. He is joined by a great army of other angels from heaven.

These men were on the bottom rung of Jewish society. Shepherds were poorly educated and had little time for religious observance as a wandering life with their flocks kept them from attending the synagogue. But the news that countless Jews through the centuries prayed for and longed to hear – the arrival of the Messiah – is given to them first!

They see not just one angel but a whole army of angels and 'the glory of the Lord shone over them'. No wonder they leave their sheep and go to the town in search of this baby. They find the newborn baby in a manger just as the angel said. Bubbling over with joy and excitement, they cannot stop praising God and telling people about what has happened.

How many people believed what the shepherds told them? We don't know. For Mary and Joseph it must have reminded them of their own angelic encounters nine months earlier.

MEDITATIO:

- Why do you think God chose to proclaim the news of Jesus' birth and reveal its significance to such lowly regarded shepherds?
- What do you think Mary and Joseph might have felt about these rough shepherds bringing this news from an angel about their newborn son? Was it a shock or perhaps a confirmation of what they already knew?
- Mary and Joseph pondered, the shepherds rejoiced, the angels sang and the crowds were amazed. How will you respond today?
- How do you tell the wonderful events to those around you when they ask why or how you celebrate Christmas?

 ORATIO:

Luke tells us that the angels invited everyone to rejoice over the birth of Jesus. Psalm 97 leads the way for us. Verses 1 and 12 are below:

> 'The Lord is King! Earth, be glad!
> All you that are righteous be glad
> Because of what the Lord has done!
> Remember what the holy God has done,
> And give thanks to him.'

Use these words to inspire your praise to God and give thanks that you too have heard the wonderful news of Jesus' birth.

 CONTEMPLATIO:

As you celebrate the birth of our Saviour today, reflect on these words from Titus 3:4-7,

> 'But when the kindness and love of God our Saviour was revealed, he saved us. It was not because of any good deeds that we ourselves had done, but because of his own mercy that he saved us, through the Holy Spirit, who gives us new birth and new life by washing us. God poured out the Holy Spirit abundantly on us through Jesus Christ our Saviour, so that by his grace we might be put right with God and come into possession of the eternal life we hope for.'

GOD'S PROTECTION

Matthew 2:13-15, 19-23

[13] After they had left, an angel of the Lord appeared in a dream to Joseph and said, "Herod will be looking for the child in order to kill him. So get up, take the child and his mother and escape to Egypt, and stay there until I tell you to leave."

[14] Joseph got up, took the child and his mother, and left during the night for Egypt, [15] where he stayed until Herod died. This was done to make what the Lord had said through the prophet come true, "I called my Son out of Egypt."

[19] After Herod died, an angel of the Lord appeared in a dream to Joseph in Egypt [20] and said, "Get up, take the child and his mother, and go back to the land of Israel, because those who tried to kill the child are dead." [21] So Joseph got up, took the child and his mother, and went back to Israel.

[22] But when Joseph heard that Archelaus had succeeded his father Herod as king of Judea, he was afraid to go there. He was given more instructions in a dream, so he went to the province of Galilee [23] and made his home in a town named Nazareth. And so what the prophets had said came true: "He will be called a Nazarene."

Other Readings: Ecclesiasticus 3:2-6, 12-14; Psalm 128:1-5; Colossians 3:12-21

 LECTIO:

The visit from the Magi is still fresh in Mary and Joseph's mind when an angel speaks to Joseph in a dream, this time giving a warning to leave the country as the family is in danger. (We'll look at the Magi's visit in more detail next Sunday.)

Herod the Great, who ruled on behalf of the Romans, was worried. His rule was harsh and at the slightest whiff of a threat to his reign, he took action. This time he is looking to kill a young king – the newborn child the Magi have told him about.

God intervenes for the Holy Family. They flee to Egypt – a journey of several hundred miles. The family leaves quickly that night and stays in Egypt living quietly until Herod's death.

God then sends his messenger to speak to Joseph again. This time the angel tells him to return home. Joseph is obedient and sets off immediately for Palestine.

But along the way Joseph realises that although Herod's kingdom had been split up, Archelaus, one of Herod's crueller sons, now runs Judea. Joseph is nervous and unsure about what to do.

A third dream helps Joseph make the decision to go to the small town of Nazareth, in the northern province of Galilee, which is ruled by Herod Antipas, who later beheads John the Baptist.

Two more prophecies are fulfilled through Joseph's obedience to God. Jesus, like Israel, is called out of exile in Egypt as prophesied by Hosea 11:1, 'I called my Son out of Egypt.' Matthew also attributes prophetic significance to Jesus being brought up in Nazareth. He may have in mind Judges 13:5-7 or Isaiah 11:1 where the Hebrew word *nezer* (which is similar to Nazarene) means branch. Isaiah says a new branch will grow out of the root of Jesse. A new beginning will emerge from the royal house of David bringing deliverance and salvation, which Jesus offered and continues to offer to everyone who will follow him.

 MEDITATIO:

- How do you think Mary and Joseph felt as they arrived in Egypt and set about finding a new home, work and an income? What can you learn from this?
- God gave Joseph specific directions that shaped human history. How do you feel God intervenes today?
- Think about the times you have experienced God's protection or guidance.
- How do you discern between your own good ideas and a word from God to direct you?

 ORATIO:

Psalm 128 commends us to fear and obey God. This fear is not about being terrified but rather a respect and holy awe for who God is. Bring some of the large and small decisions you have to make to God so he can lead you. Ask the Holy Spirit to help you act on what God tells you.

Spend some time praying for members of your family today.

 CONTEMPLATIO:

Colossians 3:12-21 speaks about relationships, firstly with God and then with our families and others. Spend some time pondering on these verses and let God speak to you through them.

A KING FOR EVERYONE

Matthew 2:1-12

¹ Jesus was born in the town of Bethlehem in Judea, during the time when Herod was king. Soon afterwards, some men who studied the stars came from the east to Jerusalem ² and asked, "Where is the baby born to be the king of the Jews? We saw his star when it came up in the east, and we have come to worship him."

³ When King Herod heard about this, he was very upset, and so was everyone else in Jerusalem. ⁴ He called together all the chief priests and the teachers of the Law and asked them, "Where will the Messiah be born?"

⁵ "In the town of Bethlehem in Judea," they answered. "For this is what the prophet wrote:

⁶ 'Bethlehem in the land of Judah,
   you are by no means the least of the leading cities of Judah;
 for from you will come a leader
   who will guide my people Israel.' "

⁷ So Herod called the visitors from the east to a secret meeting and found out from them the exact time the star had appeared. ⁸ Then he sent them to Bethlehem with these instructions: "Go and make a careful search for the child, and when you find him, let me know, so that I too may go and worship him."

⁹⁻¹⁰ And so they left, and on their way they saw the same star they had seen in the east. When they saw it, how happy they were, what joy was theirs! It went ahead of them until it stopped over the place where the child was. ¹¹ They went into the house, and when they saw the child with his mother Mary, they knelt down and worshipped him. They brought out their gifts of gold, frankincense, and myrrh, and presented them to him.

¹² Then they returned to their country by another road, since God had warned them in a dream not to go back to Herod.

Other Readings: Isaiah 60:1-6; Psalm 72:1-2, 7-8, 10-13; Ephesians 3:2-3, 5-6

 LECTIO:

Today's narrative focuses on Jesus, Herod, and 'some men who studied the stars,' or Magi, after the term in the Greek text. The fact that these men came from a distant country was another indication of the worldwide significance of Jesus' birth.

The Magi follow a new star that had appeared in the sky and arrive in Jerusalem, the seat of power for the Jews in Israel. They must have been disappointed not to find the new king here.

As they make their enquiries about this new king, people are upset. Every Jew knew that Herod would deal ruthlessly with any threat to his rule.

Herod is anxious about the Magi's search too. He takes advice from the religious leaders. The scriptures pointed towards the Messiah, a descendant of King David, being born in David's home town, Bethlehem (Micah 5:2 and 2 Samuel 5:2).

Herod invites the Magi to a secret meeting so he can learn more about the threat and tells them to report back to him after they have found the young child.

Once the Magi set out on the last stage of their journey, the star guides them again. They are full of joy. The star leads them right to Jesus, where they kneel down, worship him and present their gifts.

God knows Herod's true intentions so warns the Magi not to return to Herod but to go home by another route.

 # MEDITATIO:

- How did you find Jesus? What helped guide you to him? Did God use other people that you didn't expect?
- In what ways is Jesus your leader and guide?
- Think about the different ways you can worship Jesus. What 'gifts' can you offer him today?

 # ORATIO:

God made use of the Magi's study of the stars to lead them to Jesus. Look back at the ways God led you to Jesus and how he has guided you through your life. Thank him for each step. Now ask God about the year ahead. What priorities does he want you to set? Lay your plans and hopes before him in prayer. Ask him to guide you to do what pleases him.

 # CONTEMPLATIO:

The liturgy comments upon the mystery of the incarnation in Isaiah 60:1-6 and Ephesians 3:2-6. Spend some time reflecting on these texts and ask the Holy Spirit to reveal Jesus to you.

ANOINTED FOR MINISTRY

Matthew 3:13-17

¹³ At that time Jesus arrived from Galilee and came to John at the Jordan to be baptized by him. ¹⁴ But John tried to make him change his mind. "I ought to be baptized by you," John said, "and yet you have come to me!"

¹⁵ But Jesus answered him, "Let it be so for now. For in this way we shall do all that God requires." So John agreed.

¹⁶ As soon as Jesus was baptized, he came up out of the water. Then heaven was opened to him, and he saw the Spirit of God coming down like a dove and alighting on him. ¹⁷ Then a voice said from heaven, "This is my own dear Son, with whom I am pleased."

Other Readings: Isaiah 42:1-4, 6-7; Psalm 29:1-4, 9-10; Acts 10:34-38

 LECTIO:

Based on what we read in the Gospels, Jesus' ministry begins with his baptism by John in the river Jordan. John had been baptising the crowds for some time as a sign of repentance for their sins and turning back to God.

From the preceding verses, (Matthew 3: 10-12, which we looked at on the Second Sunday in Advent) John clearly believed the Messiah would bring in the Kingdom of heaven, and judgement with it. So there was an urgent need for repentance. The Messiah would bring a different baptism, not with water but with the Holy Spirit and fire.

So when Jesus comes humbly for water baptism John initially protests. He recognises Jesus' Messianic ministry. John is 'not good enough even to carry his sandals' (Matthew 3:11). Yet Jesus, instead of acting in power and judgement, identifies himself with everyone else who is stepping forward in repentance.

Jesus acknowledges John's objection but insists this fulfils 'all that God requires'. Through this act of obedience, Jesus demonstrates his priorities for the rest of his ministry – doing things God's way rather than his own.

After Jesus comes up out of the water he sees the Holy Spirit come down on him like a dove and stay with him. God the Father confirms that Jesus is his 'own dear Son, with whom I am well pleased'. Here we see the Holy Trinity working together in unity.

It isn't clear from Matthew's account whether others saw the vision of the dove and heard God's voice too. However, in John's Gospel it is clear that John the Baptist also saw the Spirit come down on Jesus and that God told him this meant that Jesus was the Messiah (John 1:29-34 which we will read next Sunday).

 ## MEDITATIO:

- Jesus didn't need to repent of any sins. So consider why God wanted Jesus to be baptised by John publicly along with everyone else.
- Jesus and John show us clearly that we need to obey God even when others may misunderstand our actions. Are the opinions of others hindering you from obeying God in any way? Take a few moments to reflect on this.
- Few people hear God speak to them with an audible voice or see a sign from heaven like a dove. How does God speak to you?

 ## ORATIO:

Think about how much God loves Jesus. Now think about how much God loves you —sending Jesus to die in your place so you could be adopted into his family. Take some time to give thanks to your heavenly Father.

Ask God if there is anything he wants you to do for him. Ask the Holy Spirit to help you.

 ## CONTEMPLATIO:

Jesus was empowered for his ministry by the Holy Spirit. How significant is the Holy Spirit in your relationship with God? Among other things the Holy Spirit reveals Jesus to us and equips us to serve God. Consider the work of the Holy Spirit and invite him to help and guide you.

A SAVIOUR FOR THE WORLD

John 1:29-34

[29] The next day John saw Jesus coming to him, and said, "There is the Lamb of God, who takes away the sin of the world! [30] This is the one I was talking about when I said, 'A man is coming after me, but he is greater than I am, because he existed before I was born.' [31] I did not know who he would be, but I came baptizing with water in order to make him known to the people of Israel."

[32] And John gave this testimony: "I saw the Spirit come down like a dove from heaven and stay on him. [33] I still did not know that he was the one, but God, who sent me to baptize with water, had said to me, 'You will see the Spirit come down and stay on a man; he is the one who baptizes with the Holy Spirit.' [34] I have seen it," said John, "and I tell you that he is the Son of God."

Other Readings: Isaiah 49:3, 5-6; Psalm 40:1, 3, 6-9; 1 Corinthians 1:1-3

 LECTIO:

These verses in the very first chapter of John's Gospel present John the Baptist bearing clear witness that Jesus is the long awaited Messiah.

John the Baptist was a prophet and his mission was to prepare the way for the Messiah. He preached the need for repentance from sin and a turning back to God. This was demonstrated publicly by baptism in the river Jordan.

The apostle John doesn't describe the details of Jesus' baptism like the other Gospel writers. Instead he chooses to focus on one key detail and its significance. The key point is John the Baptist's statement, 'I saw the Spirit come down like a dove from heaven and stay on him.' (verse 32).

John the Baptist goes on to explain the significance of this. God had told him that the person he saw this happen to is the 'one who baptises with the Holy Spirit', the one he was preparing the way for – the Messiah. It was this special mark of the Holy Spirit that marked Jesus out from everyone else.

God also inspires John the Baptist to proclaim that Jesus is the 'Lamb of God'. This gives us a hint that Jesus might be a rather different sort of Messiah to the one most people at the time were expecting. This Messiah was not coming to deliver the Jewish people from the Romans but to deliver them from sin and empower them to live in a new kingdom. And his mission was not just to rescue God's people in Israel but was to include the whole world.

So John points us to Jesus as the fulfilment of Isaiah's prophecy about the Suffering Servant in Isaiah 53, where in verse 7 the Suffering Servant is compared with 'a lamb about to be slaughtered'. Part of Jesus' ministry is that of the sacrificial lamb offered to God for the forgiveness of sins.

In verse 30 John the Baptist also makes another revealing comment, 'he existed before I was born'. In physical terms John was born before Jesus. In Luke 1:36 the angel Gabriel told Mary that she would give birth to Jesus and that Elizabeth, John's mother, was six months' pregnant. But the apostle John opens his Gospel by stating that Jesus existed in the Godhead before the world was created (John 1:1-3).

 MEDITATIO:

- If the presence of the Holy Spirit was essential for Jesus' ministry, what does this tell us about our need for the Holy Spirit's presence?
- What is your experience of the work of the Holy Spirit in your life?
- What can we learn about Jesus from his description as the 'Lamb of God'?

 ORATIO:

Pray through Psalm 40 and see what insights it gives you about Jesus. Then pray it again and put yourself into the psalm. Let God speak to you through it.

Give thanks that Jesus came to take away your sin so that you can enjoy fellowship and peace with God.

Thank God that Jesus is 'a light to nations so that the whole world may be saved' (Isaiah 49:6). Pray for those that Jesus lays on your heart.

 CONTEMPLATIO:

Read through Isaiah 53 and reflect on the image of God's Son as a lamb. Spend a little time with God and allow the wonder of what you are reading about Jesus to sink deep within you. Let it be a source of hope for this coming week.

A GREAT LIGHT

Matthew 4:12-23

¹² When Jesus heard that John had been put in prison, he went away to Galilee.
¹³ He did not stay in Nazareth, but went to live in Capernaum, a town by Lake
Galilee, in the territory of Zebulun and Naphtali. ¹⁴ This was done to make what
the prophet Isaiah had said come true:

¹⁵ "Land of Zebulun and land of Naphtali,
on the road to the sea, on the other side of the Jordan,
Galilee, land of the Gentiles!
¹⁶ The people who live in darkness
will see a great light.
On those who live in the dark land of death
the light will shine."

¹⁷ From that time Jesus began to preach his message: "Turn away from your sins,
because the Kingdom of heaven is near!"

¹⁸ As Jesus walked along the shore of Lake Galilee, he saw two brothers who
were fishermen, Simon (called Peter) and his brother Andrew, catching fish in the
lake with a net. ¹⁹ Jesus said to them, "Come with me, and I will teach you to catch
people." ²⁰ At once they left their nets and went with him.

²¹ He went on and saw two other brothers, James and John, the sons of Zebedee.
They were in their boat with their father Zebedee, getting their nets ready. Jesus
called them, ²² and at once they left the boat and their father, and went with him.

²³ Jesus went all over Galilee, teaching in the synagogues, preaching the Good
News about the Kingdom, and healing people who had all kinds of disease and
sickness.

Other Readings: Isaiah 8:23 – 9:3; Psalm 27:1, 4, 13-14; 1 Corinthians 1:10-13, 17

 LECTIO:

We begin with a mini geography lesson to help us understand who was where
and why. John the Baptist preached in Judea where we find both Jerusalem and
Bethlehem, in the southern part of Palestine. John ministered in the east near the
river Jordan.

Herod Antipas had John the Baptist put in prison because he publicly criticised
him for living with his brother Philip's wife, breaking Jewish law (Leviticus 18:16).
Eventually Herod's wife engineered Herod to have John put to death (Matthew 14).

Matthew doesn't explain the connection but simply says that after John's arrest Jesus moved north to Galilee. Jesus doesn't return to Nazareth where he grew up but chooses instead to live in Capernaum. Matthew interprets this as a fulfilment of Isaiah's Messianic prophecy in Isaiah 9:1-2.

At that time most of the people living in Zebulun and Naphtali were Gentiles, so by choosing to start his ministry in this region Jesus gives a clear sign of the universal nature of his mission.

In this passage Matthew tells us about two aspects of Jesus' ministry. Firstly, he preached the Good News about the Kingdom and healed people of all kinds of illness. Secondly, he calls the first four of his disciples in order to train them to 'catch people' rather than fish.

Matthew gives us very little detail about Jesus' encounter with these four fishermen. Jesus must however have made a remarkable impression on them because they were willing to leave their jobs so they could follow him.

 # MEDITATIO:

- Why do you think Peter, Andrew, James and John were prepared to leave their jobs to become Jesus' disciples?
- What qualities do you think Jesus saw in these four men that led him to choose them to be his disciples?
- What is the Good News of the Kingdom? What does it mean for you personally?
- How would you feel if Jesus appeared in your workplace? In what ways is Jesus calling you to follow him? Are you prepared to obey him, like the disciples, whatever the cost?

 # ORATIO:

Psalm 27 offers many words of encouragement, not least to hold firm to the Lord and hope in him because he is our light and stronghold. Invite the Holy Spirit to minister to you using the words of this Psalm to build faith and confidence in God.

Jesus still brings healing to broken hearts and bodies today, although we don't always understand the way he works. Ask him to help those you know who need his healing touch.

 # CONTEMPLATIO:

Consider the 'great light' in verse 16. What makes Jesus a great light for all people and for you personally?

KINGDOM PRIORITIES

Matthew 5:1-12

¹ Jesus saw the crowds and went up a hill, where he sat down. His disciples gathered round him, ² and he began to teach them:

³ "Happy are those who know they are spiritually poor;
    the Kingdom of heaven belongs to them!
⁴ Happy are those who mourn;
    God will comfort them!
⁵ Happy are those who are humble;
    they will receive what God has promised!
⁶ Happy are those whose greatest desire is to do what God requires;
    God will satisfy them fully!
⁷ Happy are those who are merciful to others;
    God will be merciful to them!
⁸ Happy are the pure in heart;
    they will see God!
⁹ Happy are those who work for peace;
    God will call them his children!
¹⁰ Happy are those who are persecuted because they do what God requires;
    the Kingdom of heaven belongs to them!

¹¹ "Happy are you when people insult you and persecute you and tell all kinds of evil lies against you because you are my followers. ¹² Be happy and glad, for a great reward is kept for you in heaven. This is how the prophets who lived before you were persecuted.

Other Readings: Zephaniah 2:3, 3:12-13; Psalm 146:7-10; 1 Corinthians 1:26-31

 LECTIO:

Scholars believe that Mark's Gospel was written before the other two synoptic gospels, enabling Matthew and Luke to draw on his material when writing their own accounts.

But Matthew and Luke also draw on other sources especially concerning the teaching of Jesus. In Matthew's Gospel Jesus' teaching is drawn together from different times and places and presented in five extensive teaching sections. Today's passage, often referred to as the Beatitudes, marks the beginning of the first of these – the Sermon on the Mount (Matthew 5:1 – 7:27).

Jesus' teaching centres on what it means to live under God's kingship on earth. So a clue to help us understand this passage appears in the prayer Jesus teaches his disciples in Matthew 6:10, 'May your Kingdom come and your will be done on earth as it is in heaven'.

Jesus' ministry is to bring God's rule to earth. God's kingdom is very different to worldly priorities and values. The worldly view is that money, success and power are good news. But here Jesus teaches that the people who are truly on the right course are those who are dependent on God and are seeking his priorities for their lives.

The word translated as ' happy' could also be translated as 'congratulations'. These are attitudes rather than moral principles. So Jesus says that if you have these attitudes – if you are humble, show mercy, are pure, work for peace, are prepared to obey God even if this involves persecution, recognise your need for God, allow God to comfort you and your greatest aim is to please God – you are lining yourself up with God's kingdom.

 # MEDITATIO:

- Each of the beatitudes is challenging. Which do you find most challenging and why?
- Which of the beatitudes seems most achievable to you and why?
- What difference would it make to our world if all Christians demonstrated these attitudes in their lives?

 # ORATIO:

Choose just one of these beatitudes and talk to Jesus about it. Ask him for the grace to be able to give God's ways more priority in your life. Remember God sends the Holy Spirit to help us live for him.

Last week we read how the apostles had to leave their everyday lives behind so they could learn how to live and minister in God's kingdom. Jesus has given us the beatitudes to enable us to do the same. Draw apart from your busy life for a little while every day this week and allow God to replenish you so that you can live out the beatitudes more faithfully.

 # CONTEMPLATIO:

Consider each of the rewards and promises God makes to those who have these attitudes. Reflect on just how wonderful and valuable they are.

SALT AND LIGHT

Matthew 5:13-16

¹³ "You are like salt for the whole human race. But if salt loses its saltiness, there is no way to make it salty again. It has become worthless, so it is thrown out and people trample on it.

¹⁴ "You are like light for the whole world. A city built on a hill cannot be hidden. ¹⁵ No one lights a lamp and puts it under a bowl; instead he puts it on the lampstand, where it gives light for everyone in the house. ¹⁶ In the same way your light must shine before people, so that they will see the good things you do and praise your Father in heaven.

Other Readings: Isaiah 58:7-10; Psalm 112:4-9; 1 Corinthians 2:1-5

 LECTIO:

We continue to reflect on Jesus' teaching for his followers. Matthew drew all these nuggets of wisdom together and created the beautiful but challenging Sermon on the Mount (Matthew 5-7). Given on different occasions, the individual lessons circulated freely around the Christian community of the first century AD.

Last week we looked at the beatitudes. Matthew chooses to follow this with three striking images that Jesus used to describe a disciple's relationship with the world.

The significance of the ideas has changed a little for us today. At the time Matthew was writing the primary role of salt was as a preservative to prevent things from going bad. While this is still important, most people today would think of using salt to improve the flavour of food.

The image of light is briefly interrupted by the image of a city on a hill. Cities were often built on hilltops because it made them easier to defend. They had influence over the surrounding area and would be highly visible.

Jesus continues to talk about light. For many of us a flick of a switch will give us as many lights as we want indoors. And it's easy to slip a torch into our pocket for a walk on a dark night. These are recent developments. In Jesus' day, little oil and rush lamps lit houses. Outside the stars and moon shone, the only other light. So light was very important. Jesus uses humour to help reinforce his message. No one would think of putting a lamp under a bowl – there would be no point and soon the light would go out completely.

This English translation uses comparisons to explain – you are like salt or light. But the original Greek makes a stronger statement, saying you *are* the salt for the whole human race and you *are* the light.

Jesus places a responsibility on Christians individually, and on the Church collectively, to be salt, light and a city set on a hill. We are to show the way, add flavour and be an example in our communities. And the purpose is that God is given praise – or as we pray in the Lord's prayer, that God's holy name is honoured.

 ## MEDITATIO:

- Consider the three images Jesus uses of salt, light and a city on a hill. What can we learn from each about living out our faith in this world?
- The readings from Isaiah 58 and Psalm 112 give some practical examples of being salt and light. Consider whether, and how, you can put any of these into practice in your life.

 ## ORATIO:

Do you feel ready for the responsibility Jesus is laying upon you as his disciple? The apostle Paul felt no shame in laying bare his own fears and anxieties before God and us (1 Corinthians 2:1-8); we need not fear doing the same. So ask God to strengthen you and give you boldness to be salt and light for him in your family, at work and in your community.

 ## CONTEMPLATIO:

When Jesus sets the standards for our Christian lives, we can easily make the mistake of trying to meet these in our own strength. Paul reminds us that we shouldn't rely on our own abilities but on the power of the spirit. Read Paul's full prayer in Ephesians 1:17-20 and let this encourage you. Verses 17, 19 and 20 are given below.

> '...and ask the God of our Lord Jesus Christ, the glorious Father, to give you the Spirit, who will make you wise and reveal God to you, so that you will know him.
> ...and how very great is his power at work in us who believe. This power working in us is the same as the mighty strength which he used when he raised Christ from death and seated him at his right side in the heavenly world.'

KINGDOM LIVING

Matthew 5:20-34, 37*

²⁰ I tell you, then, that you will be able to enter the Kingdom of heaven only if you are more faithful than the teachers of the Law and the Pharisees in doing what God requires.

²¹ "You have heard that people were told in the past, 'Do not commit murder; anyone who does will be brought to trial.' ²² But now I tell you: whoever is angry with his brother will be brought to trial, whoever calls his brother 'You good-for-nothing!' will be brought before the Council, and whoever calls his brother a worthless fool will be in danger of going to the fire of hell. ²³ So if you are about to offer your gift to God at the altar and there you remember that your brother has something against you, ²⁴ leave your gift there in front of the altar, go at once and make peace with your brother, and then come back and offer your gift to God.

²⁵ "If someone brings a lawsuit against you and takes you to court, settle the dispute with him while there is time, before you get to court. Once you are there, he will hand you over to the judge, who will hand you over to the police, and you will be put in jail. ²⁶ There you will stay, I tell you, until you pay the last penny of your fine.

²⁷ "You have heard that it was said, 'Do not commit adultery.' ²⁸ But now I tell you: anyone who looks at a woman and wants to possess her is guilty of committing adultery with her in his heart. ²⁹ So if your right eye causes you to sin, take it out and throw it away! It is much better for you to lose a part of your body than to have your whole body thrown into hell. ³⁰ If your right hand causes you to sin, cut it off and throw it away! It is much better for you to lose one of your limbs than for your whole body to go to hell.

³¹ "It was also said, 'Anyone who divorces his wife must give her a written notice of divorce.' ³² But now I tell you: if a man divorces his wife, for any cause other than her unfaithfulness, then he is guilty of making her commit adultery if she marries again; and the man who marries her commits adultery also.

³³ "You have also heard that people were told in the past, 'Do not break your promise, but do what you have vowed to the Lord to do.' ³⁴ But now I tell you: do not use any vow when you make a promise...

³⁷ Just say 'Yes' or 'No' – anything else you say comes from the Evil One.

*The full reading is Matthew 5:17-37

Other Readings: Ecclesiasticus 15:15-20; Psalm 119:1-2, 4-5, 17-18, 33-34; 1 Corinthians 2:6-10

LECTIO:

In this part of the Sermon on the Mount Jesus contrasts the demands he places on his disciples with the demands of Judaism as taught by the teachers of the Law and the Pharisees. Jesus teaches that it is not enough just to keep a code of moral and religious rules, but rather his disciples must focus on doing everything God requires.

In these few verses Jesus touches on some powerful areas – anger, disputes, lust, divorce and honesty.

Jesus' teaching illustrates the need for us to control our thoughts and emotions before they result in outward actions. He deliberately exaggerates to make his point. So removing your eye or cutting off your right hand is not to be taken literally but demonstrates how ruthlessly we must deal with sinful thoughts that can lead to sinful actions. Sin is not something we can live with. We must remove it completely, and as quickly as possible.

 # MEDITATIO:

- Jesus' teaching lays bare human frailties. Right living starts with right attitudes. Which of the areas Jesus mentions challenges you most?
- Is there anyone you need to make peace with?
- How do you deal with thoughts and emotions that can lead you into sin?

 # ORATIO:

Bring today's Gospel reading humbly before God. Allow your prayer to flow as you listen to what he says to you.

 # CONTEMPLATIO:

Slowly read today's verses from Psalm 119. Pause after each verse and meditate on it before moving onto the next one.

WALK IN LOVE

Matthew 5:38-48

³⁸ "You have heard that it was said, 'An eye for an eye, and a tooth for a tooth.' ³⁹ But now I tell you: do not take revenge on someone who wrongs you. If anyone slaps you on the right cheek, let him slap your left cheek too. ⁴⁰ And if someone takes you to court to sue you for your shirt, let him have your coat as well. ⁴¹ And if one of the occupation troops forces you to carry his pack one kilometre, carry it two kilometres. ⁴² When someone asks you for something, give it to him; when someone wants to borrow something, lend it to him.

⁴³ "You have heard that it was said, 'Love your friends, hate your enemies.' ⁴⁴ But now I tell you: love your enemies and pray for those who persecute you, ⁴⁵ so that you may become the children of your Father in heaven. For he makes his sun to shine on bad and good people alike, and gives rain to those who do good and to those who do evil. ⁴⁶ Why should God reward you if you love only the people who love you? Even the tax collectors do that! ⁴⁷ And if you speak only to your friends, have you done anything out of the ordinary? Even the pagans do that! ⁴⁸ You must be perfect – just as your Father in heaven is perfect!

Other Readings: Leviticus 19:1-2, 17-18; Psalm 103:1-4, 8, 10, 12-13;
1 Corinthians 3:16-23

 LECTIO:

This passage opens with Jesus highlighting some Old Testament teaching (Exodus 21:12-27 and its parallel texts in Leviticus). Jesus wants to contrast the guidelines set out in the Law, or the Torah, with a new attitude and way of behaving.

The Law established the level of compensation equal to the damage done – an eye for an eye and so on. Jesus points his disciples to a new way of looking at things where generosity is the standard.

For this kind of behaviour, which goes well beyond human expectations, Jesus takes God as the model. We have to imitate God, who is perfect (verse 48). God does not distinguish between good and bad people when he lavishes his blessings on mankind. In this God shows his perfection.

The Torah demands God's people to be holy and perfect just as God is (see today's reading from Leviticus). In the Gospel reading, God calls for his people to sort out disputes, not to hold grudges and to love others as themselves. What a different place this world would be if we lived like that. Well, this is indeed the challenge that Jesus places before us: follow my example.

MEDITATIO:

- Who influences your behaviour towards others, God or 'the world'?
- What lessons can we learn from this passage about the values of the kingdom? In what practical ways can we start living the kingdom way now?
- Have you been in a situation, perhaps even in church, where no one speaks to you? Jesus' words in verse 47 challenge us to be friendly to others. Look out for opportunities to speak a friendly word to people this week.

ORATIO:

'Praise the Lord, my soul, and do not forget how kind he is.
He forgives all my sins...'
'He does not punish us as we deserve or repay us
according to our sins and wrongs' Psalm 103:2-3, 10

Thank God for the mercy and grace he has shown you. If there is someone you need to forgive or are finding it hard to love, ask God to help you. Remembering God's forgiveness for you may help.

Today's passage specifically instructs us to pray for people who persecute us. Maybe someone has been unkind or hurtful to you. Bring them before the Lord and ask God how you can pray for them.

CONTEMPLATIO:

Consider the ways in which Jesus gives us an example of loving his neighbour as himself and 'turning the other cheek'.

What is true wisdom? Read 1 Corinthians 3:16-23 and think about what God considers wise.

WHO ARE YOU SERVING?

Matthew 6:24-34

[24] "No one can be a slave of two masters; he will hate one and love the other; he will be loyal to one and despise the other. You cannot serve both God and money.

[25] "This is why I tell you not to be worried about the food and drink you need in order to stay alive, or about clothes for your body. After all, isn't life worth more than food? And isn't the body worth more than clothes? [26] Look at the birds: they do not sow seeds, gather a harvest and put it in barns; yet your Father in heaven takes care of them! Aren't you worth much more than birds? [27] Can any of you live a bit longer by worrying about it?

[28] "And why worry about clothes? Look how the wild flowers grow: they do not work or make clothes for themselves. [29] But I tell you that not even King Solomon with all his wealth had clothes as beautiful as one of these flowers. [30] It is God who clothes the wild grass – grass that is here today and gone tomorrow, burnt up in the oven. Won't he be all the more sure to clothe you? How little faith you have!

[31] "So do not start worrying: 'Where will my food come from? or my drink? or my clothes?' [32] (These are the things the pagans are always concerned about.) Your Father in heaven knows that you need all these things. [33] Instead, be concerned above everything else with the Kingdom of God and with what he requires of you, and he will provide you with all these other things. [34] So do not worry about tomorrow; it will have enough worries of its own. There is no need to add to the troubles each day brings.

Other Readings: Isaiah 49:14-15; Psalm 62:1-2, 5-8; 1 Corinthians 4:1-5

 LECTIO:

Jesus seems to be saying in this text, 'tell me what you are preoccupied about and I will tell you who your master is'. In other words, if you are overly concerned about the worries of the day then they are ruling you.

Jesus makes it clear we have to make a choice. We can serve God or we can serve money and everyday concerns but we can't serve both. If we are guided by faith in God, the only master that really counts in this world, everyday worries lose their power.

Jesus also reminds us about God's nature. He is the God of creation and sustainer of life. He created beautiful flowers that are here one day then gone the next. He provides for the birds of the sky. If he takes care of birds and plants how much more will he look after people that he made in his image?

Jesus, echoing the opening phrase of the prayer he taught us (Matthew 6:9-15), refers twice to God as 'your Father in heaven'. These four words combine two immensely powerful ideas. Firstly the relationship we are invited to have with God is like a father and child. But, unlike earthly fathers with all their limitations, our spiritual Father is in heaven, perfect and all powerful.

God fully understands that as humans we need food, drink and clothing. Scripture also teaches that we should work to provide for ourselves and we should take care of those who are unable to provide for themselves.

Where people go hungry it is not God that has failed. There is enough food in the world for everyone but man's greed and selfishness mean it is not distributed fairly, which is an offence against God's providence.

 # MEDITATIO:

- Reread today's Gospel passage but imagine Jesus speaking directly to you. Does what Jesus is saying affect the way you feel? In what way? What do you need to do?
- How do we know what God requires of us in practical terms? And how do we keep our priorities right?

 # ORATIO:

Read Psalm 62 and use this as a basis for your own prayer.

Think about how God has provided for you in different ways during your life and give him thanks. Bring any worries you have before him honestly.

 # CONTEMPLATIO:

Consider God as your father in heaven. Remember his love and care and this wonderful promise he makes to his people in Isaiah 49:15,

'...I will never forget you.'

BUILD WISELY

Matthew 7:21-27

[21] "Not everyone who calls me 'Lord, Lord' will enter the Kingdom of heaven, but only those who do what my Father in heaven wants them to do. [22] When Judgement Day comes, many will say to me, 'Lord, Lord! In your name we spoke God's message, by your name we drove out many demons and performed many miracles!' [23] Then I will say to them, 'I never knew you. Get away from me, you wicked people!'

[24] "So then, anyone who hears these words of mine and obeys them is like a wise man who built his house on rock. [25] The rain poured down, the rivers overflowed, and the wind blew hard against that house. But it did not fall, because it was built on rock.

[26] "But anyone who hears these words of mine and does not obey them is like a foolish man who built his house on sand. [27] The rain poured down, the rivers overflowed, the wind blew hard against that house, and it fell. And what a terrible fall that was!"

Other Readings: Deuteronomy 11:18, 26-28, 32; Psalm 31:1-3, 16, 24; Romans 3:21-25, 28

 LECTIO:

Today's reading marks the end of Jesus' teaching on the Sermon on the Mount. It is also helpful to look at the preceding verses. In Matthew 7:13-14 Jesus teaches that people have a choice of two gates: one is narrow and the way hard, the other wide and easy. The majority choose the easy way but it leads to hell. Only a few find the path that leads to heaven. This is followed in verses 15-20 with the image of two types of tree, explaining that genuine disciples produce good fruit.

Today's text continues this theme. Jesus makes it clear that the Christian lifestyle boils down to a simple choice – obedience. It is not enough to merely read or listen to Jesus' teaching. The mark of a true disciple is doing what God asks us to do (verses 21 and 24).

Jesus speaks about a Judgement Day at the end of time for everyone, including Christians. This was not a new idea in Jesus' day, but here he wants everyone to understand the importance of discipleship to the final outcome. Jesus reveals that he himself is the judge and will make the final decision on who gets into heaven and who doesn't.

The sobering thing is that outward appearances can be deceptive. People may appear to have done amazing things for God but Jesus sees into people's hearts. He sees their true motives and whether they have put Jesus' teaching into practice in their lives.

We are back to choices again. Who makes the wise choice? The person who builds wisely on a rock will not see the storms of life wash away what he builds. How does he learn where and what to build? Like Jesus – by listening to God and obediently following his directions.

 # MEDITATIO:

- What makes someone wise according to Jesus? How wise do you consider yourself to be using this criterion?
- What do you consider are the foundations of the Christian faith? How important are they in your everyday life?
- Jesus makes it clear that we can expect 'storms' in our lives. Has your faith been tested by any 'storms' or upsets such as a sudden bereavement or the loss of a job or other event?
- What sustains your faith in times of testing?

 # ORATIO:

Read Romans 3:21-25 and 28. These verses remind us that our salvation is a free gift from God based entirely on his grace and made possible through the death and resurrection of Jesus.

Living out our lives in obedience to God's mercy is a true disciple's response. Ask God to help you obey him and live a life that pleases him.

 # CONTEMPLATIO:

Jesus says, 'Whoever loves me will obey my teaching. My Father will love him, and my Father and I will come to him and live with him' (John 14:23). Take some time to reflect on this verse.

OVERCOMING TEMPTATION

Matthew 4:1-11

[1] Then the Spirit led Jesus into the desert to be tempted by the Devil. [2] After spending 40 days and nights without food, Jesus was hungry. [3] Then the Devil came to him and said, "If you are God's Son, order these stones to turn into bread."

[4] But Jesus answered, "The scripture says, 'Human beings cannot live on bread alone, but need every word that God speaks.'"

[5] Then the Devil took Jesus to Jerusalem, the Holy City, set him on the highest point of the Temple, [6] and said to him, "If you are God's Son, throw yourself down, for the scripture says:

'God will give orders to his angels about you;
they will hold you up with their hands,
so that not even your feet will be hurt on the stones.'"

[7] Jesus answered, "But the scripture also says, 'Do not put the Lord your God to the test.'"

[8] Then the Devil took Jesus to a very high mountain and showed him all the kingdoms of the world in all their greatness. [9] "All this I will give you," the Devil said, "if you kneel down and worship me."

[10] Then Jesus answered, "Go away, Satan! The scripture says, 'Worship the Lord your God and serve only him!'"

[11] Then the Devil left Jesus; and angels came and helped him.

Other Readings: Genesis 2:7-9, 3:1-7; Psalm 51:1-4, 10-12, 15; Romans 5:12-19

 ## LECTIO:

The events we read about today happened early in Jesus' ministry and were under God's control, as verse 1 makes clear.

The Holy Spirit leads Jesus on his divine mission, into the desert. He stays there for forty days and fasts the whole time. Forty is significant as a time of preparation in the Old Testament. It recalls Moses fasting forty days on Mount Sinai (Exodus 34:28) and the Israelites spending forty years in the wilderness before entering the Promised Land (Deuteronomy 8:2-3, 29:5-6).

Matthew only tells us about three specific temptations. In the first, the Devil tempts Jesus to use his supernatural power to meet his own physical need. Jesus rejects him, identifying with us; we need more than just physical food. The implication is clear that we also need 'spiritual food' from God.

Next, the Devil tempts Jesus to prove his divine nature by throwing himself off the temple so God will send his angels to rescue him.

Lastly, he offers to give Jesus power over the nations if he will worship him. Jesus really had come to save people from the Devil's control, but not this way.

These three examples illustrate the core of every temptation: the desire to push God aside, to regard him as secondary and redundant, relying solely on one's own strength, and to put the world right without God.

The Devil's cunning deceptions don't deceive Jesus, even when he uses scripture itself (Psalm 91:11-12) to tempt him. Jesus in turn rejects every temptation with scripture, quoting successively from Deuteronomy 8:3, 6:16 and 6:13. Authentic interpretation of a portion of scripture must be consistent with the whole of scripture.

The essence of all temptation is the offer of an appealing alternative to God's way of doing things. This is true for Jesus and for us.

 ## MEDITATIO:

- What helped Jesus overcome these temptations? What lessons can we learn to help us overcome the temptations we face?
- What do you think Jesus means when he quotes from Deuteronomy 8:3 in Matthew 4:4. Do you consider God's Word an essential part of your daily food? How do you let God's Word nourish you?
- What are the day-to-day temptations that you face?

 ## ORATIO:

'Create a pure heart in me, O God,
and put a new and loyal spirit in me.
Give me again the joy that comes from your salvation,
and make me willing to obey you.' Psalm 51:10, 12

Psalm 51 offers us a way to come before God in repentance and ask for his forgiveness. Read the whole Psalm and allow your own prayer to flow to God.

 ## CONTEMPLATIO:

As we start this season of Lent we look forward to Jesus' victory on the cross over sin so we can enjoy salvation living. Meditate on these wonderful words from Romans 5:15, 17,

'...but God's grace is much greater,...
All who receive God's abundant grace and are freely put right with him
will rule in life through Christ.'

GOD'S CHOSEN ONE

Matthew 17:1-9

¹ Six days later Jesus took with him Peter and the brothers James and John and led them up a high mountain where they were alone. ² As they looked on, a change came over Jesus: his face was shining like the sun, and his clothes were dazzling white. ³ Then the three disciples saw Moses and Elijah talking with Jesus. ⁴ So Peter spoke up and said to Jesus, "Lord, how good it is that we are here! If you wish, I will make three tents here, one for you, one for Moses, and one for Elijah."

⁵ While he was talking, a shining cloud came over them, and a voice from the cloud said, "This is my own dear Son, with whom I am pleased – listen to him!"

⁶ When the disciples heard the voice, they were so terrified that they threw themselves face downwards on the ground. ⁷ Jesus came to them and touched them. "Get up," he said. "Don't be afraid!" ⁸ So they looked up and saw no one there but Jesus.

⁹ As they came down the mountain, Jesus ordered them, "Don't tell anyone about this vision you have seen until the Son of Man has been raised from death."

Other Readings: Genesis 12:1-4; Psalm 33:4-5, 18-20, 22; 2 Timothy 1:8-10

 LECTIO:

Jesus chooses only his first three disciples – Peter, John and James – to climb a mountain with him for a prayer time. And the disciples witness something remarkable.

The first thing they notice is Jesus' face shining. Then they spot his clothes have turned dazzling white. Next, he is talking with Moses and Elijah.

The appearance of these two men, both major figures in Israel's history, is significant. Moses led the exodus of God's people out of slavery in Egypt. And many Jews expected the prophet Elijah to return before the coming of the Messiah.

In Luke's account (Luke 9:31) the prophets talk with Jesus about how he will soon fulfil God's purpose through his death (or 'exodus', the literal meaning of the word Luke uses) in Jerusalem. Jesus will fulfil God's salvation plan for humankind, bringing everlasting deliverance.

This breath-taking experience may have strengthened Jesus. He faced many testing days ahead, days that ended with his death on the cross. The shining cloud reveals God's presence and veils his glory. As at Jesus' baptism, God speaks. He affirms Jesus as his Son whom he has chosen. And this time God adds the instruction to the disciples to 'listen to him'.

This event, together with the other miracles and teaching that surround it, should have enlightened the disciples. But they needed to travel much further with Jesus. In fact, it wasn't until they met him after the resurrection that they really understood who he was and his God-given mission on earth.

 # MEDITATIO:

- What range of feelings or emotions do you think the disciples experienced?
- God says of Jesus, "This is my own dear Son, with whom I am pleased—listen to him!" What do you think the three disciples would have made of this?
- Why do you think Jesus told them not to discuss this vision with anyone until after they saw the Son of Man raised from the dead?
- Where has God appeared veiled by a cloud before?

 # ORATIO:

'The words of the Lord are true,
and all his works are dependable. ...
May your constant love be with us, Lord,
as we put our hope in you.' Psalm 33:4, 22

How easy do you find it to listen to God? Read through Psalm 33. You may simply want to focus on a few verses like the two above. Ask God to speak to you. Then make your response to him in prayer.

 # CONTEMPLATIO:

'He saved us and called us to be his own people, not because of what we have done, but because of his own purpose and grace.' 2 Timothy 1:9

In the reading from 2 Timothy 1:8-10 the apostle Paul encourages us not to be ashamed of witnessing for our Lord or suffering for the Good News. Consider your response to this.

LIFE-GIVING WATER

John 4:5-15, 25-26, 39, 41-42*

[5] In Samaria he came to a town named Sychar, which was not far from the field that Jacob had given to his son Joseph. [6] Jacob's well was there, and Jesus, tired out by the journey, sat down by the well. It was about noon.

[7] A Samaritan woman came to draw some water, and Jesus said to her, "Give me a drink of water." [8] (His disciples had gone into town to buy food.)

[9] The woman answered, "You are a Jew, and I am a Samaritan – so how can you ask me for a drink?" (Jews will not use the same cups and bowls that Samaritans use.)

[10] Jesus answered, "If only you knew what God gives and who it is that is asking you for a drink, you would ask him, and he would give you life-giving water."

[11] "Sir," the woman said, "you haven't got a bucket, and the well is deep. Where would you get that life-giving water? [12] It was our ancestor Jacob who gave us this well; he and his sons and his flocks all drank from it. You don't claim to be greater than Jacob, do you?"

[13] Jesus answered, "All those who drink this water will be thirsty again, [14] but whoever drinks the water that I will give him will never be thirsty again. The water that I will give him will become in him a spring which will provide him with life-giving water and give him eternal life."

[15] "Sir," the woman said, "give me that water! Then I will never be thirsty again, nor will I have to come here to draw water."

[25] The woman said to him, "I know that the Messiah will come, and when he comes, he will tell us everything."

[26] Jesus answered, "I am he, I who am talking with you."

[39] Many of the Samaritans in that town believed in Jesus because the woman had said…, "He told me everything I have ever done."… [41] Many more believed because of his message, [42] and they said to the woman, "We believe now, not because of what you said, but because we ourselves have heard him, and we know that he really is the Saviour of the world."

*The full reading is John 4:5-42, this is a shortened version.

Other Readings: Exodus 17:3-7; Psalm 95:1-2, 6-9; Romans 5:1-2, 5-8

LECTIO:

Today we stand by the well as Jesus talks to a Samaritan woman. John is the only Gospel writer to tell us about this dramatic encounter.

The Jews took a very dim view of the Samaritans. At the time it wouldn't have been culturally acceptable for a man to be alone with a woman unless they were married or related. So it was doubly unusual for Jesus to speak to this Samaritan woman alone.

Life for this woman has been tough and she is living with a man who is not her husband. Her previous husbands may have divorced her; it was easy, they just had to write a letter of divorce and the marriage was history.

But Jesus' words touched her and his knowledge of her life struck home. She took up the offer of everlasting water instantly. And, unable to keep this amazing encounter to herself, she ran to tell others in the town to come and meet Jesus.

 # MEDITATIO:

- This woman had experienced a lot of rejection and judgement in her life. Jesus chooses to speak to her on her own. What does this reveal about his respect for her as an individual? What can we learn from this?
- This woman would have been looked down upon in her community. Why do you think Jesus chose to reveal himself as the Messiah to her?
- Make your own response to Jesus' offer of life-giving water.
- In what ways can you invite others to meet Jesus?

 # ORATIO:

Every time we pray we can have a personal conversation with Jesus just like this Samaritan woman. God loves you and cares for you, whatever your situation. Open your heart up to God in prayer now. The living water – the life that Jesus offers – is for you too.

 # CONTEMPLATIO:

Jesus met this woman at the well. Sit with a glass of water and as you sip it allow God to speak to you. Spend some time reflecting on the true worship that Jesus is looking for (verse 23).

ONE THING I DO KNOW

John 9:1, 6-9, 13-17, 34-36*

[1] As Jesus was walking along, he saw a man who had been born blind.

[6] After he said this, Jesus spat on the ground and made some mud with the spittle; he rubbed the mud on the man's eyes [7] and said, "Go and wash your face in the Pool of Siloam." (This name means "Sent".) So the man went, washed his face, and came back seeing.

[8] His neighbours, then, and the people who had seen him begging before this, asked, "Isn't this the man who used to sit and beg?"

[9] Some said, "He is the one," but others said, "No he isn't; he just looks like him."

So the man himself said, "I am the man."

[13] Then they took to the Pharisees the man who had been blind. [14] The day that Jesus made the mud and cured him of his blindness was a Sabbath. [15] The Pharisees, then, asked the man again how he had received his sight. He told them, "He put some mud on my eyes; I washed my face, and now I can see."

[16] Some of the Pharisees said, "The man who did this cannot be from God, for he does not obey the Sabbath law."

Others, however, said, "How could a man who is a sinner perform such miracles as these?" And there was a division among them.

[17] So the Pharisees asked the man once more, "You say he cured you of your blindness – well, what do you say about him?"

"He is a prophet," the man answered.

[34] They answered, "You were born and brought up in sin – and you are trying to teach us?" And they expelled him from the synagogue.

[35] When Jesus heard what had happened, he found the man and asked him, "Do you believe in the Son of Man?"

[36] The man answered, "Tell me who he is, sir, so that I can believe in him!"

*This is a shortened form of today's reading. The full reading is John 9:1-41.

Other Readings: 1 Samuel 16:1, 6-7, 10-13; Psalm 23; Ephesians 5:8-14

 LECTIO:

We know from the earlier chapters in John's Gospel that Jesus was not popular with the Pharisees. They were watching him closely, looking for any opportunity to accuse him.

Such an opportunity presents itself when a man is brought before them who Jesus has healed on the Sabbath. This is not the first time Jesus has crossed the Jewish authorities by healing on the Sabbath (see John 5:1-18).

The Pharisees strictly observed the law which didn't permit any work on the Sabbath (Exodus 23:12, 31:12-17). Jesus observed the Sabbath too but disagreed with the Pharisees on what constituted 'work'. Healing, in Jesus' opinion, was doing good and bringing praise to God – truly honouring the Sabbath.

This blind man has a rollercoaster of a time. Imagine his joy at being able to see for the very first time in his life! But instead of being able to celebrate, things get complicated. Some people doubt him (verse 9). The Pharisees finally believe him after his parents confirm he was born blind but end up expelling him from the synagogue (verse 34).

Physical healing is wonderful but an even greater healing is still to come. Jesus searches for the man, revealing himself as the Son of Man and inviting him to believe. The man confesses his faith in Jesus and his spiritual blindness is cured too.

 # MEDITATIO:

- Consider how Jesus treated this man. Compare this with the Pharisees' response. What can we learn from this?
- In 1 Samuel 16:7 we are told that God looks at the heart and not outward appearances. How does this relate to our Gospel reading? Do we make judgements about people based on their appearance or social status?
- The Pharisees thought they were doing what God wanted but ended up working against God. How can we avoid doing this ourselves?
- Have you met God in such a way that you feel confident enough in your own spiritual experience to be able to stand your ground when others question you?

 # ORATIO:

Psalm 23 can resonate on many levels. Focus on a couple of verses each day this week and make them your personal prayer.

Pray for those you know who need physical and spiritual healing.

 # CONTEMPLATIO:

Do you remember when God first invited you to believe in him? Consider the ways God's grace has worked in your life right up to today.

RESURRECTION LIFE

John 11:3-7, 17, 20-27, 33-45*

³ The sisters sent Jesus a message: "Lord, your dear friend is ill."

⁴ When Jesus heard it, he said, "The final result of this illness will not be the death of Lazarus; this has happened in order to bring glory to God, and it will be the means by which the Son of God will receive glory."

⁵ Jesus loved Martha and her sister and Lazarus. ⁶ Yet when he received the news that Lazarus was ill, he stayed where he was for two more days. ⁷ Then he said to the disciples, "Let us go back to Judea."

¹⁷ When Jesus arrived, he found that Lazarus had been buried four days before.

²⁰ When Martha heard that Jesus was coming, she went out to meet him, but Mary stayed in the house. ²¹ Martha said to Jesus, "If you had been here, Lord, my brother would not have died! ²² But I know that even now God will give you whatever you ask him for."

²³ "Your brother will rise to life," Jesus told her.

²⁴ "I know," she replied, "that he will rise to life on the last day."

²⁵ Jesus said to her, "I am the resurrection and the life. Those who believe in me will live, even though they die; ²⁶ and all those who live and believe in me will never die. Do you believe this?"

²⁷ "Yes, Lord!" she answered. "I do believe that you are the Messiah, the Son of God, who was to come into the world."

³³ Jesus saw her weeping, and he saw how the people who were with her were weeping also; his heart was touched, and he was deeply moved. ³⁴ "Where have you buried him?" he asked them.

"Come and see, Lord," they answered.

³⁵ Jesus wept. ³⁶ "See how much he loved him!" the people said.

³⁷ But some of them said, "He gave sight to the blind man, didn't he? Could he not have kept Lazarus from dying?"

³⁸ Deeply moved once more, Jesus went to the tomb, which was a cave with a stone placed at the entrance. ³⁹ "Take the stone away!" Jesus ordered.

Martha, the dead man's sister, answered, "There will be a bad smell, Lord. He has been buried four days!"

⁴⁰ Jesus said to her, "Didn't I tell you that you would see God's glory if you believed?" ⁴¹ They took the stone away. Jesus looked up and said, "I thank you, Father, that you listen to me. ⁴² I know that you always listen to me, but I say this for the sake of the people here, so that they will believe that you sent me." ⁴³ After he had said this, he called out in a loud voice, "Lazarus, come out!" ⁴⁴ He came

out, his hands and feet wrapped in grave clothes, and with a cloth round his face. "Untie him," Jesus told them, "and let him go."

[45] Many of the people who had come to visit Mary saw what Jesus did, and they believed in him.

This is a shortened form of today's reading. The full reading is John 11:1-45.

Other Readings: Ezekiel 37:12-14; Psalm 130; Romans 8:8-11

 # LECTIO:

Mary and Martha are very close friends of Jesus so they are dismayed when he appears to arrive too late – after their brother has died.

From the outset Jesus is aware that his Father has a glorious plan (verse 4) but that still doesn't prevent him from sharing their grief (verses 33-35).

Jesus declares 'I am the resurrection and the life' and promises that those who believe in him will never die (verses 25-26). Martha expresses her faith that Jesus is the promised Messiah.

Jesus raises Lazarus from the dead so that people will believe he is the Son of God. Many people do believe but for the religious leaders Jesus now poses so great a threat that they plot to kill him (verse 53).

 # MEDITATIO:

- What things strike you most from this story?
- What does this miracle demonstrate about Jesus' authority?
- 'I am the resurrection and the life.' What does this statement mean for you? What do you think about eternal life?

 # ORATIO:

Respond to God in prayer. Bring your hopes and fears to him and thank him for his loving care.

 # CONTEMPLATIO:

Read Romans 8:8-11 and let these verses strengthen your faith and confidence in God's promises.

WHO IS HE?

Matthew 21:1-11

[1] As Jesus and his disciples approached Jerusalem, they came to Bethphage at the Mount of Olives. There Jesus sent two of the disciples on ahead [2] with these instructions: "Go to the village there ahead of you, and at once you will find a donkey tied up with her colt beside her. Untie them and bring them to me. [3] And if anyone says anything, tell him, 'The Master needs them'; and then he will let them go at once."

[4] This happened in order to make what the prophet had said come true:

[5] "Tell the city of Zion,

   Look, your king is coming to you!

He is humble and rides on a donkey

   and on a colt, the foal of a donkey."

[6] So the disciples went and did what Jesus had told them to do: [7] they brought the donkey and the colt, threw their cloaks over them, and Jesus got on. [8] A large crowd of people spread their cloaks on the road while others cut branches from the trees and spread them on the road. [9] The crowds walking in front of Jesus and those walking behind began to shout, "Praise to David's Son! God bless him who comes in the name of the Lord! Praise God!"

[10] When Jesus entered Jerusalem, the whole city was thrown into an uproar. "Who is he?" the people asked.

[11] "This is the prophet Jesus, from Nazareth in Galilee," the crowds answered.

Other Readings: Isaiah 50:4-7; Psalm 22:7-8, 16-19, 22-23; Philippians 2:6-11

 LECTIO:

We begin Holy Week with Jesus' triumphant entry into Jerusalem. What an occasion it must have been, loaded with symbolic images and meaning.

Jesus' starting point, the Mount of Olives, is significant as it is associated in scripture with the coming of the Lord (Zechariah 14:4).

Matthew begins by describing the remarkable provision of a donkey and colt for Jesus to ride on. The disciples follow Jesus' instructions and return with the animals that he had told them they would find. Matthew (verse 4) interprets this as the fulfilment of Zechariah's prophecy (Zechariah 9:9-10) proclaiming a King who comes as Saviour on a lowly colt, not with powerful horses and chariots. Jesus is fully in control and aware of what his last few days on earth will bring.

People spread their cloaks on the road before Jesus, a customary greeting for a victorious king or important person (2 Kings 9:13). They shout, 'God bless him who comes in the name of the Lord' (verse 9), echoing the words of Psalm 118:25-26.

Jesus' dramatic entrance couldn't have come at a worse time for the Pharisees. Jerusalem was packed with pilgrims who had come to celebrate the Passover (Luke 22:7). Matthew tells us, 'When Jesus entered Jerusalem, the whole city was thrown into uproar. "Who is he?" the people asked.' (verse 10).

The Pharisees didn't accept Jesus or his teaching and wanted to prevent others from following him. Nothing could be worse than this noisy, public, hero's welcome. They may have feared, with good reason, the brutal intervention of the Roman soldiers to restore public order.

His followers believed Jesus to be the Messiah; the religious leaders didn't believe him and many were undecided. And people's responses to Jesus still vary today. Who is Jesus – a prophet, a healer, a good teacher or is he the Messiah, the Son of God?

 MEDITATIO:

- 'Who is he?' This was the crucial question when Jesus entered Jerusalem and it continues to be the crucial question for every single person ever since. What do you believe and why?
- What can we learn from the actions of the disciples in this passage?
- What does the way Jesus entered Jerusalem reveal to us about him and his mission?

 ORATIO:

Use Philippians 2:6-11 to give thanks to God for his willingness to send his Son to leave heaven, become a man and die on the cross for our sins. Bow before him in worship and extol the 'name that is greater than any other name'.

 CONTEMPLATIO:

Jesus died to save you so that you can spend all eternity rejoicing in his presence. Have you invited him to be Lord of your life? Are there elements of Jesus' teaching you still resist and are unwilling to accept? Is there more you need to surrender to God today?

A SERVANT HEART

John 13:1-15

[1] It was now the day before the Passover Festival. Jesus knew that the hour had come for him to leave this world and go to the Father. He had always loved those in the world who were his own, and he loved them to the very end.

[2] Jesus and his disciples were at supper. The Devil had already put into the heart of Judas, the son of Simon Iscariot, the thought of betraying Jesus. [3] Jesus knew that the Father had given him complete power; he knew that he had come from God and was going to God. [4] So he rose from the table, took off his outer garment, and tied a towel round his waist. [5] Then he poured some water into a basin and began to wash the disciples' feet and dry them with the towel round his waist. [6] He came to Simon Peter, who said to him, "Are you going to wash my feet, Lord?"

[7] Jesus answered him, "You do not understand now what I am doing, but you will understand later."

[8] Peter declared, "Never at any time will you wash my feet!"

"If I do not wash your feet," Jesus answered, "you will no longer be my disciple."

[9] Simon Peter answered, "Lord, do not wash only my feet, then! Wash my hands and head, too!"

[10] Jesus said, "Those who have had a bath are completely clean and do not have to wash themselves, except for their feet. All of you are clean – all except one." [11] (Jesus already knew who was going to betray him; that is why he said, "All of you, except one, are clean.")

[12] After Jesus had washed their feet, he put his outer garment back on and returned to his place at the table. "Do you understand what I have just done to you?" he asked. [13] "You call me Teacher and Lord, and it is right that you do so, because that is what I am. [14] I, your Lord and Teacher, have just washed your feet. You, then, should wash one another's feet. [15] I have set an example for you, so that you will do just what I have done for you.

Other Readings: Exodus 12:1-8, 11-14; Psalm 116:12-13, 15-18; 1 Corinthians 11:23-26

 LECTIO:

These events are set within the context of the Passover meal. Our Old Testament reading (Exodus 12:1-8, 11-14) reminds us of the huge significance this feast had for Jews. It was a feast remembering God's miraculous deliverance of his people.

John is the only gospel writer to give us this precious example of Jesus washing the disciples' feet.

Jesus' actions must have stunned the disciples. Normally the host provided water for guests entering the house to wash their own feet (Luke 7:44). Sometimes a servant or slave might attend to the task. Very occasionally, disciples might wash their teacher's feet. But never the other way round. This is unprecedented.

Peter protests strongly but then submits even though he still misunderstands Jesus' purpose and wants complete purification. In this practical action, Jesus demonstrates a very important lesson to the disciples and to us – we must serve one another just as he serves us. Humility and servanthood are marks of true discipleship.

What Jesus is really looking for is humility – the only doorway to the gift of salvation. We cannot gain salvation by our own actions; only accepting the humble sacrifice of the Son of God on the cross can redeem us.

MEDITATIO:

- Imagine Jesus washing your feet. How would you feel? What would you say to him?
- How willing are you to follow Jesus' example and serve others? In what practical ways can you do this?
- Judas sat at the table and no doubt allowed Jesus to wash his feet. So Jesus humbled himself before his betrayer (verse 11). What does this tell us about Jesus, and indeed about Judas too?

ORATIO:

Make Psalm 116 your prayer for the next day or two. Consider Jesus' feelings and actions as you read these words. Listen to what the Holy Spirit might say to you and consider the words of the Psalmist in verse 12,

> 'What can I offer the Lord for all his goodness to me?'

CONTEMPLATIO:

Reflect on Christ's love, humility and painful death for us. Consider too his never ending desire to draw us into fellowship with the Trinity.

GREATER LOVE HAS NO MAN

John 18:1 – 19:42
John 18

¹ After Jesus had said this prayer, he left with his disciples and went across the brook called Kidron. There was a garden in that place, and Jesus and his disciples went in. ² Judas, the traitor, knew where it was, because many times Jesus had met there with his disciples. ³ So Judas went to the garden, taking with him a group of Roman soldiers, and some temple guards sent by the chief priests and the Pharisees; they were armed and carried lanterns and torches. ⁴ Jesus knew everything that was going to happen to him, so he stepped forward and asked them, "Who is it you are looking for?"

⁵ "Jesus of Nazareth," they answered.

"I am he," he said.

Judas, the traitor, was standing there with them. ⁶ When Jesus said to them, "I am he," they moved back and fell to the ground. ⁷ Again Jesus asked them, "Who is it you are looking for?"

"Jesus of Nazareth," they said.

⁸ "I have already told you that I am he," Jesus said. "If, then, you are looking for me, let these others go." ⁹ (He said this so that what he had said might come true: "Father, I have not lost even one of those you gave me.")

¹⁰ Simon Peter, who had a sword, drew it and struck the High Priest's slave, cutting off his right ear. The name of the slave was Malchus. ¹¹ Jesus said to Peter, "Put your sword back in its place! Do you think that I will not drink the cup of suffering which my Father has given me?"

¹² Then the Roman soldiers with their commanding officer and the Jewish guards arrested Jesus, bound him, ¹³ and took him first to Annas. He was the father-in-law of Caiaphas, who was High Priest that year. ¹⁴ It was Caiaphas who had advised the Jewish authorities that it was better that one man should die for all the people.

¹⁵ Simon Peter and another disciple followed Jesus. That other disciple was well known to the High Priest, so he went with Jesus into the courtyard of the High Priest's house, ¹⁶ while Peter stayed outside by the gate. Then the other disciple went back out, spoke to the girl at the gate, and brought Peter inside. ¹⁷ The girl at the gate said to Peter, "Aren't you also one of the disciples of that man?"

"No, I am not," answered Peter.

¹⁸ It was cold, so the servants and guards had built a charcoal fire and were standing round it, warming themselves. So Peter went over and stood with them, warming himself.

¹⁹ The High Priest questioned Jesus about his disciples and about his teaching.

²⁰ Jesus answered, "I have always spoken publicly to everyone; all my teaching was done in the synagogues and in the Temple, where all the people come together.

I have never said anything in secret. [21] Why, then, do you question me? Question the people who heard me. Ask them what I told them – they know what I said."

[22] When Jesus said this, one of the guards there slapped him and said, "How dare you talk like that to the High Priest!"

[23] Jesus answered him, "If I have said anything wrong, tell everyone here what it was. But if I am right in what I have said, why do you hit me?"

[24] Then Annas sent him, still bound, to Caiaphas the High Priest.

[25] Peter was still standing there keeping himself warm. So the others said to him, "Aren't you also one of the disciples of that man?"

But Peter denied it. "No, I am not," he said.

[26] One of the High Priest's slaves, a relative of the man whose ear Peter had cut off, spoke up. "Didn't I see you with him in the garden?" he asked.

[27] Again Peter said "No" – and at once a cock crowed.

[28] Early in the morning Jesus was taken from Caiaphas' house to the governor's palace. The Jewish authorities did not go inside the palace, for they wanted to keep themselves ritually clean, in order to be able to eat the Passover meal. [29] So Pilate went outside to them and asked, "What do you accuse this man of?"

[30] Their answer was, "We would not have brought him to you if he had not committed a crime."

[31] Pilate said to them, "Then you yourselves take him and try him according to your own law."

They replied, "We are not allowed to put anyone to death." [32] (This happened in order to make the words of Jesus come true, the words he used when he indicated the kind of death he would die.)

[33] Pilate went back into the palace and called Jesus. "Are you the King of the Jews?" he asked him.

[34] Jesus answered, "Does this question come from you or have others told you about me?"

[35] Pilate replied, "Do you think I am a Jew? It was your own people and the chief priests who handed you over to me. What have you done?"

[36] Jesus said, "My kingdom does not belong to this world; if my kingdom belonged to this world, my followers would fight to keep me from being handed over to the Jewish authorities. No, my kingdom does not belong here!"

[37] So Pilate asked him, "Are you a king, then?"

Jesus answered, "You say that I am a king. I was born and came into the world for this one purpose, to speak about the truth. Whoever belongs to the truth listens to me."

[38] "And what is truth?" Pilate asked.

Then Pilate went back outside to the people and said to them, "I cannot find any reason to condemn him. [39] But according to the custom you have, I always set free a prisoner for you during the Passover. Do you want me to set free for you the King of the Jews?"

⁴⁰ They answered him with a shout, "No, not him! We want Barabbas!" (Barabbas was a bandit.)

John 19

¹ Then Pilate took Jesus and had him whipped. ² The soldiers made a crown out of thorny branches and put it on his head; then they put a purple robe on him ³ and came to him and said, "Long live the King of the Jews!" And they went up and slapped him.

⁴ Pilate went out once more and said to the crowd, "Look, I will bring him out here to you to let you see that I cannot find any reason to condemn him." ⁵ So Jesus came out, wearing the crown of thorns and the purple robe. Pilate said to them, "Look! Here is the man!"

⁶ When the chief priests and the temple guards saw him, they shouted, "Crucify him! Crucify him!"

Pilate said to them, "You take him, then, and crucify him. I find no reason to condemn him."

⁷ The crowd answered back, "We have a law that says he ought to die, because he claimed to be the Son of God."

⁸ When Pilate heard this, he was even more afraid. ⁹ He went back into the palace and asked Jesus, "Where do you come from?"

But Jesus did not answer. ¹⁰ Pilate said to him, "You will not speak to me? Remember, I have the authority to set you free and also to have you crucified."

¹¹ Jesus answered, "You have authority over me only because it was given to you by God. So the man who handed me over to you is guilty of a worse sin."

¹² When Pilate heard this, he tried to find a way to set Jesus free. But the crowd shouted back, "If you set him free, that means that you are not the Emperor's friend! Anyone who claims to be a king is a rebel against the Emperor!"

¹³ When Pilate heard these words, he took Jesus outside and sat down on the judge's seat in the place called "The Stone Pavement". (In Hebrew the name is "Gabbatha".) ¹⁴ It was then almost noon of the day before the Passover. Pilate said to the people, "Here is your king!"

¹⁵ They shouted back, "Kill him! Kill him! Crucify him!"

Pilate asked them, "Do you want me to crucify your king?"

The chief priests answered, "The only king we have is the Emperor!"

¹⁶ Then Pilate handed Jesus over to them to be crucified.

So they took charge of Jesus. ¹⁷ He went out, carrying his cross, and came to "The Place of the Skull", as it is called. (In Hebrew it is called "Golgotha".) ¹⁸ There they crucified him; and they also crucified two other men, one on each side, with Jesus between them. ¹⁹ Pilate wrote a notice and had it put on the cross. "Jesus of Nazareth, the King of the Jews", is what he wrote. ²⁰ Many people read it, because the place where Jesus was crucified was not far from the city. The notice was written in Hebrew, Latin, and Greek. ²¹ The chief priests said to Pilate, "Do not write 'The

King of the Jews', but rather, 'This man said, I am the King of the Jews.' "

²² Pilate answered, "What I have written stays written."

²³ After the soldiers had crucified Jesus, they took his clothes and divided them into four parts, one part for each soldier. They also took the robe, which was made of one piece of woven cloth without any seams in it. ²⁴ The soldiers said to one another, "Let's not tear it; let's throw dice to see who will get it." This happened in order to make the scripture come true:

"They divided my clothes among themselves and gambled for my robe."

And this is what the soldiers did.

²⁵ Standing close to Jesus' cross were his mother, his mother's sister, Mary the wife of Clopas, and Mary Magdalene. ²⁶ Jesus saw his mother and the disciple he loved standing there; so he said to his mother, "He is your son."

²⁷ Then he said to the disciple, "She is your mother." From that time the disciple took her to live in his home.

²⁸ Jesus knew that by now everything had been completed; and in order to make the scripture come true, he said, "I am thirsty."

²⁹ A bowl was there, full of cheap wine; so a sponge was soaked in the wine, put on a stalk of hyssop, and lifted up to his lips. ³⁰ Jesus drank the wine and said, "It is finished!"

Then he bowed his head and died.

³¹ Then the Jewish authorities asked Pilate to allow them to break the legs of the men who had been crucified, and to take the bodies down from the crosses. They requested this because it was Friday, and they did not want the bodies to stay on the crosses on the Sabbath, since the coming Sabbath was especially holy. ³² So the soldiers went and broke the legs of the first man and then of the other man who had been crucified with Jesus. ³³ But when they came to Jesus, they saw that he was already dead, so they did not break his legs. ³⁴ One of the soldiers, however, plunged his spear into Jesus' side, and at once blood and water poured out. ³⁵ (The one who saw this happen has spoken of it, so that you also may believe. What he said is true, and he knows that he speaks the truth.) ³⁶ This was done to make the scripture come true: "Not one of his bones will be broken." ³⁷ And there is another scripture that says, "People will look at him whom they pierced."

³⁸ After this, Joseph, who was from the town of Arimathea, asked Pilate if he could take Jesus' body. (Joseph was a follower of Jesus, but in secret, because he was afraid of the Jewish authorities.) Pilate told him he could have the body, so Joseph went and took it away. ³⁹ Nicodemus, who at first had gone to see Jesus at night, went with Joseph, taking with him about 30 kilogrammes of spices, a mixture of myrrh and aloes. ⁴⁰ The two men took Jesus' body and wrapped it in linen with the spices according to the Jewish custom of preparing a body for burial.

⁴¹ There was a garden in the place where Jesus had been put to death, and in it there was a new tomb where no one had ever been buried. ⁴² Since it was the day before the Sabbath and because the tomb was close by, they placed Jesus' body there.

GREATER LOVE HAS NO MAN

John 18:1 – 19:42

Other Readings: Isaiah 52:13-53:12; Psalm 31:1, 5, 11-12, 14-16, 24;
Hebrews 4:14-16, 5:7-9

 ## LECTIO:

John's account of Jesus' passion begins with his betrayal and arrest at night. Judas leads the Roman soldiers and temple guards to a garden where Jesus often met with his disciples. However John makes it clear that Jesus is not taken by surprise and does not seek to evade his arrest, 'Jesus knew everything that was going to happen to him, so he stepped forward...' (18:4).

Jesus is taken before Annas and Caiaphas the High Priest. John doesn't give as much detail as the other gospel writers about Jesus' trial before the Jewish authorities (see Matthew 26:57-67, Mark 14:53-65, Luke 22:54-55, 63-71) but notes it was Caiaphas who advised the Jewish authorities that 'it was better that one man should die for all the people' (18:14).

The Jewish authorities have passed their sentence but require Roman permission to implement it. So they take Jesus to Pilate, who finds no reason to sentence Jesus to death. In fact he says this to the people no fewer than three times (18:38, 19:4, 6) and tries to release Jesus. But when the crowd openly call into question Pilate's allegiance to the Emperor he gives in and hands Jesus over to be crucified.

John also includes some details not found in the other three Gospels. One of these is an instruction from Jesus on the cross to 'the disciple he loved' – this is traditionally regarded as a reference to John himself – to look after his mother (John 19:26-27). He alone records Jesus' tender words and care for his mother.

Another such detail is the description of the soldier piercing Jesus' side with a spear instead of breaking his legs as in the case of the other two men crucified with him (19:32-34). John explains, 'this was done to make the scripture come true', referring to Zechariah 12:10.

We learn also that when Jesus' side was pierced 'blood and water poured out'. On a literal level this is conclusive proof that Jesus was dead, answering sceptics who later tried to deny the resurrection on the basis that Jesus was not actually dead. Some also suggest that on a symbolic level the blood and water represent Holy Eucharist or Holy Communion and baptism.

After Jesus is crucified Joseph of Arimathea asks Pilate if he can bury Jesus. Pilate gives his permission and Joseph, along with Nicodemus, prepares Jesus' body for burial and then buries him in a new tomb (19:38-40). They were both important Jewish council members and secret disciples of Jesus. John is the only gospel writer to mention Nicodemus' involvement here. He also records the meeting between Jesus and Nicodemus in John 3 which includes one of the Bible's most famous verses, John 3:16,

'For God loved the world so much that he gave his only Son, so that everyone who believes in him may not die but have eternal life.'

 # MEDITATIO:

- What do we learn about Jesus from this Passion narrative? What touches you most and why?
- In answering Pilate Jesus says, 'I was born and came into the world for this one purpose, to speak about the truth. Whoever belongs to the truth listens to me.' (18:37). What is the 'truth' Jesus is speaking about? Are you continuing to listen to Jesus?
- Jesus endured the pain and humiliation of death on the cross. What difference does this make to the way you live your life?
- What did Jesus mean when he said, 'it is finished'? What is the significance of this for you today?

 # ORATIO:

Prayerfully read Isaiah 52:13–53:12. Worship the suffering servant who was pierced for our faults and crushed for our sins. Give thanks for all Jesus accomplished on the cross for you. Surrender your burdens and sins to the loving Lord who paid the price so you can be free.

 # CONTEMPLATIO:

'Let us have confidence, then, and approach God's throne, where there is grace. There we will receive mercy and find grace to help us just when we need it.' Hebrews 4:16

Read Hebrews 4:14-16 and 5:7-9. These verses encourage and strengthen us to 'hold firmly to the faith' (verse 14).

Meditate on Jesus our high priest who understands our human weaknesses but lived on earth without sin and is 'the source of eternal salvation for all those who obey him' (verse 9).

FILLED WITH JOY

Matthew 28:1-10

[1] After the Sabbath, as Sunday morning was dawning, Mary Magdalene and the other Mary went to look at the tomb. [2] Suddenly there was a violent earthquake; an angel of the Lord came down from heaven, rolled the stone away, and sat on it. [3] His appearance was like lightning, and his clothes were white as snow. [4] The guards were so afraid that they trembled and became like dead men.

[5] The angel spoke to the women. "You must not be afraid," he said. "I know you are looking for Jesus, who was crucified. [6] He is not here; he has been raised, just as he said. Come here and see the place where he was lying. [7] Go quickly now, and tell his disciples, 'He has been raised from death, and now he is going to Galilee ahead of you; there you will see him!' Remember what I have told you."

[8] So they left the tomb in a hurry, afraid and yet filled with joy, and ran to tell his disciples.

[9] Suddenly Jesus met them and said, "Peace be with you." They came up to him, took hold of his feet, and worshipped him. [10] "Do not be afraid," Jesus said to them. "Go and tell my brothers to go to Galilee, and there they will see me."

Other Readings: Romans 6:3-11; Psalm 118:1-2, 16-17, 22-23

 LECTIO:

This is Matthew's resurrection narrative, where we learn of Jesus' victory, how he overcame death and sin forever when he died on the cross for us. We have the victory now, though our bodily resurrection won't happen until the end of time.

In a few simple words, Matthew describes the moment when the women discover Jesus is alive. These words speak volumes. Threaded through every simple word is the wonder the women must have experienced at discovering Jesus alive.

Matthew sets the scene – there was an earthquake and then an angel descended from heaven and rolled the massive stone away. The guards look on trembling with fear and become like 'dead men'. They were probably frozen with fear, unable to speak or move.

The two women go to the tomb perhaps as a focus for their grief and to mourn. They are not expecting to meet a living Jesus at all – far from it.

Knowing how frightened the two women must be the angel tells them not to be afraid and explains that Jesus is no longer dead but has been raised back to life, just as he said he would be.

The angel shows them the empty tomb and sends them on their way back to the disciples to give them the dramatic news – Jesus has risen from the dead!

On the way to tell the disciples they meet Jesus face to face. They are the first witnesses of the empty tomb and its real meaning. The tomb was not empty because someone had desecrated it and stolen Jesus' body. It was empty because Jesus had risen from the dead.

In the verses after our reading (verses 11-15) we learn that the guards report what they had seen to the chief priests who assemble an emergency meeting. They offer the soldiers a large sum of money as a bribe to keep quiet about what they really saw. Instead they lie and say that the disciples stole Jesus' body during the night while they were asleep.

 MEDITATIO:

- As you celebrate this wonderful day in the life of the church try to imagine just how amazed and excited the two women must have been when Jesus met them.
- Think about the first time Jesus came 'alive' for you. Has your faith and wonder in Jesus' resurrection grown or diminished over the years?
- Consider the contrast between the two women and the guards. Both witnessed the most significant event in human history. The women proclaim the good news. The guards lie to conceal it. What can we learn from this?

 ORATIO:

Faith in the resurrection of Jesus is a fundamental part of our Christian faith. Pray through Romans 6:3-11 asking God to bring these promises to life in your heart and experience.

 CONTEMPLATIO:

How would you summarise the Easter events for a friend who wants to know the real significance of Easter? Try jotting down the details to help sort out the important facts and remember them.

MEETING THE RISEN CHRIST

John 20:19-31

[19] It was late that Sunday evening, and the disciples were gathered together behind locked doors, because they were afraid of the Jewish authorities. Then Jesus came and stood among them. "Peace be with you," he said. [20] After saying this, he showed them his hands and his side. The disciples were filled with joy at seeing the Lord. [21] Jesus said to them again, "Peace be with you. As the Father sent me, so I send you." [22] Then he breathed on them and said, "Receive the Holy Spirit. [23] If you forgive people's sins, they are forgiven; if you do not forgive them, they are not forgiven."

[24] One of the twelve disciples, Thomas (called the Twin), was not with them when Jesus came. [25] So the other disciples told him, "We have seen the Lord!"

Thomas said to them, "Unless I see the scars of the nails in his hands and put my finger on those scars and my hand in his side, I will not believe."

[26] A week later the disciples were together again indoors, and Thomas was with them. The doors were locked, but Jesus came and stood among them and said, "Peace be with you." [27] Then he said to Thomas, "Put your finger here, and look at my hands; then stretch out your hand and put it in my side. Stop your doubting, and believe!"

[28] Thomas answered him, "My Lord and my God!"

[29] Jesus said to him, "Do you believe because you see me? How happy are those who believe without seeing me!"

[30] In his disciples' presence Jesus performed many other miracles which are not written down in this book. [31] But these have been written in order that you may believe that Jesus is the Messiah, the Son of God, and that through your faith in him you may have life.

Other Readings: Acts 2:42-47; Psalm 118:2-4, 13-15, 22-24; 1 Peter 1:3-9

 LECTIO:

In the Synoptic Gospels and in John's Gospel, we find descriptions of a number of meetings between the disciples and the risen Christ. The entire faith of the Church is based upon the testimony of those who met Jesus alive after having seen him die on the cross. The apostle Paul strongly defends Jesus' physical resurrection in response to doubts among the Christians in Corinth (1 Corinthians 15).

Jesus' resurrection confirmed all he had said and done. It also assured the disciples' faith in Jesus as the Son of God.

Thomas is not present when Jesus appears to the other disciples and he is not willing to accept their testimony. He wants to see Jesus for himself and touch his wounds. Jesus graciously allows Thomas to come to faith in his resurrection on his own terms. But Jesus is mindful of the majority of Christians who believe in his resurrection through the gift of faith, the testimony of God's word and the simple witness of other Christians who daily say, 'we believe that Jesus died and rose again'.

In this passage Jesus also commissions the disciples to continue his mission of restoring people into right relationship with God and extending God's kingdom rule on earth, saying, 'As the Father sent me, so I send you.' This is followed immediately with the gift of the Holy Spirit.

The passage ends with a clear declaration of faith. Real life is only possible lived out through faith in Jesus.

MEDITATIO:

- Have you encountered the risen Christ and accepted his lordship and divinity? How did you come to accept Jesus as your Lord and God?
- Is your faith in Jesus something that is only formal or intellectual? How does it affect your daily life?
- What do you feel Jesus has sent you to do? What part can the Holy Spirit play in this?

ORATIO:

Prayerfully offer your life to God, especially the areas that you find difficult to surrender to his Lordship. Pray the words 'Jesus, My Lord and God' as you submit each area to him.

CONTEMPLATIO:

Three times in this passage Jesus says to his disciples 'Peace be with you'. We all need to hear these words. God's peace keeps our hearts and minds safe (Philippians 4:7). Take some time to be renewed by God's peace.

OPENED EYES

Luke 24:13-35

¹³On that same day two of Jesus' followers were going to a village named Emmaus, about 11 kilometres from Jerusalem, ¹⁴and they were talking to each other about all the things that had happened. ¹⁵As they talked and discussed, Jesus himself drew near and walked along with them; ¹⁶they saw him, but somehow did not recognize him. ¹⁷Jesus said to them, "What are you talking about to each other, as you walk along?"

They stood still, with sad faces. ¹⁸One of them, named Cleopas, asked him, "Are you the only visitor in Jerusalem who doesn't know the things that have been happening there these last few days?"

¹⁹"What things?" he asked.

"The things that happened to Jesus of Nazareth," they answered. "This man was a prophet and was considered by God and by all the people to be powerful in everything he said and did. ²⁰Our chief priests and rulers handed him over to be sentenced to death, and he was crucified. ²¹And we had hoped that he would be the one who was going to set Israel free! Besides all that, this is now the third day since it happened. ²²Some of the women of our group surprised us; they went at dawn to the tomb, ²³but could not find his body. They came back saying they had seen a vision of angels who told them that he is alive. ²⁴Some of our group went to the tomb and found it exactly as the women had said, but they did not see him."

²⁵Then Jesus said to them, "How foolish you are, how slow you are to believe everything the prophets said! ²⁶Was it not necessary for the Messiah to suffer these things and then to enter his glory?" ²⁷And Jesus explained to them what was said about himself in all the Scriptures, beginning with the books of Moses and the writings of all the prophets.

²⁸As they came near the village to which they were going, Jesus acted as if he were going farther; ²⁹but they held him back, saying, "Stay with us; the day is almost over and it is getting dark." So he went in to stay with them. ³⁰He sat down to eat with them, took the bread, and said the blessing; then he broke the bread and gave it to them. ³¹Then their eyes were opened and they recognized him, but he disappeared from their sight. ³²They said to each other, "Wasn't it like a fire burning in us when he talked to us on the road and explained the Scriptures to us?"

³³They got up at once and went back to Jerusalem, where they found the eleven disciples gathered together with the others ³⁴and saying, "The Lord is risen indeed! He has appeared to Simon!"

³⁵The two then explained to them what had happened on the road, and how they had recognized the Lord when he broke the bread.

Other Readings: Acts 2:14, 22-23; Psalm 16:1-2, 5, 7-11; 1 Peter 1:17-21

LECTIO:

It is the third day after Jesus' death. The tomb is open and Jesus' body is missing. Despite Jesus' promise that he would rise on the third day these two disciples seem to have given up hope and leave for Emmaus.

Jesus joins them but they do not recognise him. He explains how the Messiah's death and resurrection are essential to God's purposes and have been revealed in the scriptures. It is only when he breaks bread with them that their eyes are opened.

They rush back to Jerusalem to tell the other disciples. They arrive to find that Jesus has also appeared to Simon. So at this point in Luke's account there are three eyewitnesses to the risen Christ. Many more will join them before Jesus ascends to heaven.

 # MEDITATIO:

- Jesus revealed himself to these two disciples when they were discouraged. What can we learn from this?
- What other lessons can you learn from this passage?

 # ORATIO:

Thank Jesus that he has paid the price for your sin through his death and resurrection. Invite him to come alongside you and reveal more of himself to you. Pray for those you know who are feeling discouraged or have doubts about their faith.

 # CONTEMPLATIO:

The two disciples walked about 11 kilometres back to Jerusalem, mostly at night, to encourage their fellow disciples. Consider your response to the good news of the gospel and how you can share it with others.

LISTEN TO THE SHEPHERD

John 10:1-10

[1] Jesus said, "I am telling you the truth: the man who does not enter the sheepfold by the gate, but climbs in some other way, is a thief and a robber. [2] The man who goes in through the gate is the shepherd of the sheep. [3] The gatekeeper opens the gate for him; the sheep hear his voice as he calls his own sheep by name, and he leads them out. [4] When he has brought them out, he goes ahead of them, and the sheep follow him, because they know his voice. [5] They will not follow someone else; instead, they will run away from such a person, because they do not know his voice."

[6] Jesus told them this parable, but they did not understand what he meant.

[7] So Jesus said again, "I am telling you the truth: I am the gate for the sheep. [8] All others who came before me are thieves and robbers, but the sheep did not listen to them. [9] I am the gate. Whoever comes in by me will be saved; they will come in and go out and find pasture. [10] The thief comes only in order to steal, kill, and destroy. I have come in order that you might have life – life in all its fullness.

Other Readings: Acts 2:14, 36-41; Psalm 23:1-6; 1 Peter 2:20-25

 LECTIO:

To help us understand this passage more clearly we also need to read the following verses in John 10:11-18. In verses 1-5 Jesus tells the parable of the shepherd. He explains the meaning in verses 7-16.

Jesus uses two 'I am' statements with two metaphors to describe himself. In verse 7 he describes himself as 'the gate' and in verse 11 he refers to himself as the 'good shepherd'.

The people listening to Jesus would have been familiar with the idea of God as the shepherd and the Jewish people as his sheep. So in identifying himself as the good shepherd, Jesus identifies himself directly with God and his role in protecting and caring for his sheep.

Jesus adds that the shepherd knows each of his sheep by name and leads them. The sheep recognise his voice so they follow him out of the sheepfold, presumably to pastures where they can be fed. In verses 11-16 Jesus alludes to the fact that he will one day lay down his life for the sake of his flock. He also refers to 'other sheep', possibly Gentile converts, which will be added to form one flock.

In addition to being the good shepherd Jesus also describes himself as the gate for the sheep. The gate is the only legitimate way into the sheepfold. It is only through Jesus that we can become part of God's flock. This is summed up in John 14:6, 'I am the way, the truth, and the life; no one goes to the Father except by me.' (We will look at this passage further next Sunday.)

Jesus also compares his mission with that of false prophets and 'messiahs'. The latter steal, kill and destroy. By glorious contrast Jesus brings life – 'life in all its fullness' (verse 10).

 # MEDITATIO:

- Why do you think Jesus used these two metaphors to describe himself? What does each metaphor tell you about him?
- What have you learnt about Jesus and your relationship with him today?
- Do you see Jesus as your shepherd? When do you experience him leading you? What spiritual food and water does he provide for you?
- Do you need to make any changes to allow you to hear your shepherd's voice more clearly in the future?

 # ORATIO:

Psalm 23 is probably the best known of all the Psalms. Read through it verse by verse and use it as a personal prayer to God.

 # CONTEMPLATIO:

Reflect on this verse from 1 Peter 2:25,

'You were like sheep that had lost their way, but now you have been brought back to follow the Shepherd and Keeper of your souls.'

THE WAY

John 14:1-12

[1] "Do not be worried and upset," Jesus told them. "Believe in God and believe also in me. [2] There are many rooms in my Father's house, and I am going to prepare a place for you. I would not tell you this if it were not so. [3] And after I go and prepare a place for you, I will come back and take you to myself, so that you will be where I am. [4] You know the way that leads to the place where I am going."

[5] Thomas said to him, "Lord, we do not know where you are going; so how can we know the way to get there?"

[6] Jesus answered him, "I am the way, the truth, and the life; no one goes to the Father except by me. [7] Now that you have known me," he said to them, "you will know my Father also, and from now on you do know him and you have seen him."

[8] Philip said to him, "Lord, show us the Father; that is all we need."

[9] Jesus answered, "For a long time I have been with you all; yet you do not know me, Philip? Whoever has seen me has seen the Father. Why, then, do you say, 'Show us the Father'? [10] Do you not believe, Philip, that I am in the Father and the Father is in me? The words that I have spoken to you," Jesus said to his disciples, "do not come from me. The Father, who remains in me, does his own work. [11] Believe me when I say that I am in the Father and the Father is in me. If not, believe because of the things I do. [12] I am telling you the truth: those who believe in me will do what I do – yes, they will do even greater things, because I am going to the Father.

Other Readings: Acts 6:1-7; Psalm 33:1-2, 4-5, 18-19; 1 Peter 2:4-9

 LECTIO:

This conversation takes place about the time of the Passover meal in Jerusalem. Jesus knows that his imminent arrest and crucifixion will be a severe trial for his disciples.

Jesus doesn't say so explicitly but verses 2-4 seem to be referring to heaven. Jesus knows that after his crucifixion he will rise from the dead and join his Father in heaven.

The promise for his disciples is that after they die they too will join him in heaven, but Jesus doesn't make this plain.

Jesus' answer to Thomas – that he is the way, the truth, the life and the only way to the Father – probably didn't make things any clearer for them at the time.

In his exchange with Philip, Jesus focuses on his unity with God the Father. This is a difficult concept for the disciples to understand. In fact, it has taken centuries of the Church's meditation and reflection to scratch the surface of the mystery of the Trinity. But Jesus points out that whoever has seen Jesus has seen the Father: in Jesus we can see what God the Father is like.

Our reading ends today with Jesus' intriguing statement that his followers will do greater things than he does. This is linked to the gift of the Holy Spirit which we will read more about in the coming weeks.

It is helpful to remind ourselves of the advice Jesus gives his disciples right at the outset of this conversation:

'Do not be worried and upset...believe in God and believe also in me'.

 # MEDITATIO:

- How is Jesus the way, the truth, the life and the only way to the Father?
- How has Jesus proved to be the way for you personally? How does this affect your everyday life?
- What can we learn from this passage about trusting in God? How can you apply this in your daily life?

 # ORATIO:

Psalm 33 speaks about God's faithfulness. Read the whole Psalm and then respond to him in prayer. Like the disciples we don't always understand everything but we can be confident that God is faithful and good.

 # CONTEMPLATIO:

Consider these verses below from 1 Peter 2:4-6. Think about Jesus as the cornerstone of God's Kingdom. Ask God how you can be a 'living stone' in his temple.

> 'Come to the Lord, the living stone rejected by people as worthless but chosen by God as valuable. Come as living stones, and let yourselves be used in building the spiritual temple, where you will serve as holy priests to offer spiritual and acceptable sacrifices to God through Jesus Christ. For the scripture says,
>
> > "I chose a valuable stone,
> > which I am placing as the cornerstone in Zion;
> > and whoever believes in him will never be disappointed."'

A PRICELESS GIFT

John 14:15-21

[15] "If you love me, you will obey my commandments. [16] I will ask the Father, and he will give you another Helper, who will stay with you for ever. [17] He is the Spirit who reveals the truth about God. The world cannot receive him, because it cannot see him or know him. But you know him, because he remains with you and is in you.

[18] "When I go, you will not be left all alone; I will come back to you. [19] In a little while the world will see me no more, but you will see me; and because I live, you also will live. [20] When that day comes, you will know that I am in my Father and that you are in me, just as I am in you.

[21] "Those who accept my commandments and obey them are the ones who love me. My Father will love those who love me; I too will love them and reveal myself to them."

Other Readings: Acts 8:5-8, 14-17; Psalm 66:1-7, 16, 20; 1 Peter 3:15-18

 LECTIO:

This reading from John takes us right to the heart of the Passover supper and Jesus' final instructions for his most intimate friends and disciples.

Jesus has some important points to make about his relationship with the disciples and what will happen when he goes away and the Father sends the Holy Spirit to them.

The Holy Spirit will come with an important guarantee, his permanent presence with every disciple (verses 16-17). The world, or non-believers, cannot receive the Holy Spirit because they cannot see or know him. But the disciples will. The Holy Spirit is called 'another Helper', that is in addition to Jesus himself.

In many ways the world stands in opposition to the disciples and Jesus but John chooses not to develop that theme here.

Jesus doesn't go into any details about his return but leaves the disciples with the promise that 'I will come back for you'. So his resurrection and return is promised here in verse 18. These verses reveal the deep concern Jesus has for his beloved disciples in the face of the coming storm.

Woven throughout this lesson in love is Jesus' invitation to his disciples to live out their love for him. But he knows the disciples need all the help they can get. So Jesus turns to his Father to ask for the gift of the Holy Spirit on behalf of his disciples.

The Holy Spirit loves those who love Jesus and who keep his commandments. He also acts as advocate, helper and teacher, sustaining the disciples along the sometimes challenging path of obedience to Jesus and his commandments.

All these themes are woven into a rich tapestry of teaching. In these few verses, which are part of a much longer passage of teaching, complex ideas are spelt out with great simplicity and clarity.

 # MEDITATIO:

- The Holy Spirit has various roles but Jesus pinpoints perhaps the most important in verse 17, to reveal 'the truth about God'. We constantly need to be reminded about what God is really like because our view of God can so easily be distorted. Love and obedience will flow more easily the deeper our understanding of God's nature. Take some time to reflect on this.
- What part does the Holy Spirit play in your relationship with God? What do you do to sustain this relationship? When are you most aware of the Holy Spirit's guidance?

 # ORATIO:

The liturgy today uses Psalm 66, or part of it, to sing God's praises. Use some verses from this psalm to praise God, or maybe speak or write your own song of praise. Alternatively, try drawing a simple picture to express your praise.

Reflect on the events of the last week. Praise God for his presence with you throughout all that has happened, whether good or bad.

 # CONTEMPLATIO:

Which of the themes in today's teaching particularly touched your heart and spirit? Ask the Holy Spirit to show you what God wants you to see and how you need to respond.

THE GREAT COMMISSION

Matthew 28:16-20

[16] The eleven disciples went to the hill in Galilee where Jesus had told them to go. [17] When they saw him, they worshipped him, even though some of them doubted. [18] Jesus drew near and said to them, "I have been given all authority in heaven and on earth. [19] Go, then, to all peoples everywhere and make them my disciples: baptize them in the name of the Father, the Son, and the Holy Spirit, [20] and teach them to obey everything I have commanded you. And I will be with you always, to the end of the age."

Other Readings: Acts 1:1-11; Psalm 47:1-2, 5-8; Ephesians 1:17-23

 ## LECTIO:

These are the final words of the Gospel of Matthew. They complement the narrative in Matthew 10, when Jesus sends the twelve disciples out, as a training exercise, on their first short mission.

The two texts in chapters 10 and 28 are best read together in order to get to grips with what the early disciples understood when Jesus sent them out with their great commission. In the first commission the disciples' mission is limited to 'the lost sheep of the people of Israel' and they are specifically told not to visit Gentile territory or Samaritan towns. But after the resurrection the restrictions are removed and Jesus instructs his disciples to share the good news with all peoples everywhere.

This encounter has all the characteristics of a resurrection narrative: a meeting in a chosen place between Jesus and his chosen disciples; and a mixed reaction as some doubted they were seeing the Lord while others worshipped. In this account there is no mention of Jesus proving he is real and not a ghost; the focus is on the task ahead for the disciples.

Jesus states that he has been given 'all authority in heaven and earth' and the implication is clear that his is a God-given authority. Based on this authority, he tells the disciples to go 'to all peoples everywhere'.

His commission involved evangelising all people of the world and 'making them my disciples'. Discipleship is entered into through baptism in the name of the Trinity –'the Father, the Son, and the Holy Spirit'. Believers become members of a church, though this word is not used. Then begins the process of teaching these new disciples to understand and live the teachings Jesus gave in the years before his passion and death.

At this point, Jesus does not give the disciples a list of instructions on how to carry out the commission, but as we read in Acts 1 the Holy Spirit is poured out to enable the disciples to fulfil the mission.

The Gospel ends with a promise: Jesus will be with them until the end of time. Jesus doesn't spell out how, he simply gives the assurance. His promise, like his message, is for us today and it is eternal.

 # MEDITATIO:

- What do you understand by the great commission?
- Who do you see around you taking part in the great commission?
- How do you play your part in achieving the commission?
- How does Jesus fulfil his promise to be with us today?

 # ORATIO:

Go deeper into the power and wonder of the great commission by prayerfully reading Acts 1:1-11. Ask God to speak to you about someone with whom you can share Jesus' words. Remember Jesus promises to be with us and has sent the Holy Spirit to help us.

 # CONTEMPLATIO:

Read Ephesians 1:17-23 slowly several times and soak up these amazing verses. Verse 17 echoes what we read last week in John 14:17 about the role of the Holy Spirit in revealing God to us so that we know him.

Take a few moments to reflect on the authority that has been given to Jesus and let this strengthen your faith:

> 'Christ rules there above all heavenly rulers, authorities, powers, and lords; he has a title superior to all titles of authority in this world and in the next. God put all things under Christ's feet and gave him to the church as supreme Lord over all things.' Ephesians 1:21-22

GIFT OF THE HOLY SPIRIT

John 20:19-23

[19] It was late that Sunday evening, and the disciples were gathered together behind locked doors, because they were afraid of the Jewish authorities. Then Jesus came and stood among them. "Peace be with you," he said. [20] After saying this, he showed them his hands and his side. The disciples were filled with joy at seeing the Lord. [21] Jesus said to them again, "Peace be with you. As the Father sent me, so I send you." [22] Then he breathed on them and said, "Receive the Holy Spirit. [23] If you forgive people's sins, they are forgiven; if you do not forgive them, they are not forgiven."

Other Readings: Acts 2:1-11; Psalm 104:1, 24, 29-31, 34; 1 Corinthians 12:3-7, 12-13

 LECTIO:

Though the Feast we are celebrating is Pentecost Sunday, which occurs about fifty days after Easter Sunday, our Gospel reading today focuses on an encounter with the Holy Spirit on the very day Jesus rose from the dead.

It is the third day after Jesus' death. The disciples are afraid of the Jewish authorities so they keep a very low profile, hiding away behind locked doors.

The rest of our text tells what the risen Jesus says and does next. He greets them all by saying, 'Peace be with you', a normal greeting among the Jews. He says nothing about his ordeal or the fact that the disciples abandoned him after his arrest.

Then he shows them his hands and side, still bearing the visible signs of his crucifixion; his resurrected body still bore the marks of his suffering. Jesus probably intended to show that he was real – changed and yet the same. The signs of his suffering made it plain he was not a ghost; he lived and stood among them.

Then comes the commission, or mission (verse 21), which is almost a continuation of his own mission from the Father. Surprisingly, we discover the disciples are despatched to bring forgiveness of sins rather than to preach. Although reconciliation with God through repentance and forgiveness is of course the very essence of the Gospel.

Christian churches interpret verse 21 differently but for the Catholic Church this is the basis of the Church's authority to forgive sins after they have been confessed. Jesus gives no description of how the Church is to organise the dispensation of forgiveness. Nor is there any indication of the rite the Church was to set up. Jesus only says if the Church forgives the sins of men and women then so will God. And if the Church denies this pardon, then God will not forgive the sins either.

Through its long history, the Catholic Church has administered this sacrament in various ways. But at all times it is God's gift given to an individual in need of forgiveness administered through the Church.

But before giving this commission Jesus breathes on the disciples and says 'Receive the Holy Spirit'. So this authority should only be exercised through the power and guidance of the Holy Spirit.

 # MEDITATIO:

- Picture the scene, the disciples hidden away from the prying eyes of the world. They are scared. Fear hangs in the air and suddenly there is Jesus standing in the room. Think about what this encounter must have meant for the disciples.
- Consider the parallel between Jesus breathing on the disciples to receive the Holy Spirit and God breathing life into man at Creation (Genesis 2:7).
- How do you feel about Jesus giving the Church the authority to forgive sins?

 # ORATIO:

Ask the Holy Spirit to shine his loving light into your heart and to guide you as you seek forgiveness for your sins, perhaps in confession. These words from 1 John 1:9 offer encouragement:

'But if we confess our sins to God, he will keep his promise and do what is right, he will forgive us our sins and purify us from all our wrongdoing'.

Ask the Holy Spirit to help you live a life that is pleasing to God.

 # CONTEMPLATIO:

Read Acts 2:1-11 and try to imagine the scene when the Holy Spirit came in power on the disciples and thousands were added to the church in one day.

Then read 1 Corinthians 12 and consider the work of the Holy Spirit in your life today.

FOR GOD SO LOVED

John 3:16-18

¹⁶ For God loved the world so much that he gave his only Son, so that everyone who believes in him may not die but have eternal life. ¹⁷ For God did not send his Son into the world to be its judge, but to be its saviour.

¹⁸ Those who believe in the Son are not judged; but those who do not believe have already been judged, because they have not believed in God's only Son.

Other Readings: Exodus 34:4-6, 8-9; Daniel 3:52-56; 2 Corinthians 13:11-13

 LECTIO:

These few verses are among the best known in the Bible. For some these words have opened the doorway into life as a Christian believer.

As we take a closer look at them it is actually not at all clear who is speaking here, and the Greek text can be interpreted in different ways. It could be Jesus himself continuing his conversation with Nicodemus (verses 1-13) or it could be the gospel writer adding his own comments.

The two preceding verses help to deepen our appreciation of this text. They refer to the Son of Man being lifted up so that everyone who believes in him may have eternal life. ('Lift up' has two meanings, referring both to the cross and to Jesus' ascension to heaven.) A direct reference is made to the account in Numbers 21:6-9 where the Israelites sinned and were punished by poisonous snakes. Moses intercedes for them and God instructs him to make a snake and put it on a pole. Those who looked on the bronze snake were healed and their lives saved. The symbol of the snake on a pole remains a symbol of healing in some countries today and is used by various medical organisations. The parallel is clear: all human beings are smitten with a deadly disease but there is a cure – believing in Jesus and his victory over sin on the cross.

These verses give us a wonderful insight into God the Father and the Son. God is not indifferent to the plight of people as some believe. He loves us and demonstrated his love through his Son's birth on earth and death on the cross. This is repeated in 2 Peter 3:9, '...he wants everyone to turn from sin and no one to be lost.' (CEV).

Jesus' primary purpose is to bring salvation rather than judgement; nevertheless, we will be judged by our response to him. Believing and following Jesus causes us to live in the light. But those who choose to remain in darkness have to bear the consequences.

MEDITATIO:

- How do these verses speak to you?
- Take some time to reflect on God's love for you personally and indeed for everyone. How do you respond to this?
- How might you explain these verses to someone who is interested in becoming a Christian?

 ORATIO:

'The Lord God came down in a cloud and stood beside Moses there on the mountain. God spoke his holy name, "the Lord." Then he passed in front of Moses and called out, "I am the Lord God. I am merciful and very patient with my people. I show great love, and I can be trusted. I keep my promises to my people forever, but I also punish anyone who sins..." Exodus 34:5-7 (Contemporary English Version)

Respond to God in worship and thanksgiving. Ask the Holy Spirit to reveal any sin you need to confess. Intercede for those who need to receive God's love and forgiveness.

 CONTEMPLATIO:

Reflect on the following verses from 1 John 4:10-14. What do you think about them?

'This is what love is: it is not that we have loved God, but that he loved us and sent his Son to be the means by which our sins are forgiven.

Dear friends, if this is how God loved us, then we should love one another. No one has ever seen God, but if we love one another, God lives in union with us, and his love is made perfect in us.

We are sure that we live in union with God and that he lives in union with us, because he has given us his Spirit. And we have seen and tell others that the Father sent his Son to be the Saviour of the world.'

LIVING BREAD

John 6:51-58

[51] I am the living bread that came down from heaven. If anyone eats this bread, he will live for ever. The bread that I will give him is my flesh, which I give so that the world may live."

[52] This started an angry argument among them. "How can this man give us his flesh to eat?" they asked.

[53] Jesus said to them, "I am telling you the truth: if you do not eat the flesh of the Son of Man and drink his blood, you will not have life in yourselves. [54] Those who eat my flesh and drink my blood have eternal life, and I will raise them to life on the last day. [55] For my flesh is the real food; my blood is the real drink. [56] Those who eat my flesh and drink my blood live in me, and I live in them. [57] The living Father sent me, and because of him I live also. In the same way whoever eats me will live because of me. [58] This, then, is the bread that came down from heaven; it is not like the bread that your ancestors ate. They later died, but those who eat this bread will live for ever."

Other Readings: Deuteronomy 8:2-3, 14-16; Psalm 147:12-15, 19-20; 1 Corinthians 10:16-17

 LECTIO:

John chapter 6 opens with Jesus miraculously providing physical bread (and fish) for over 5,000 people. In the synagogue the next day Jesus teaches extensively on the living bread sent by God to give eternal life.

Today's Gospel reading comes at the end of this teaching and focuses on the 'Eucharist'. Strictly speaking, the term 'Eucharist' means 'giving thanks' and it refers to the ceremony held on the Lord's Day (Sunday) when the consecrated bread and wine is received. Catholics believe that when the words of blessing or consecration are pronounced over the bread and wine they become the body and blood of Christ. Other Christians understand it differently, seeing this as a symbol of remembrance of the Last Supper.

Catholics describe the change of the bread and wine into the Body and Blood of Christ as 'transubstantiation'. It is a 'mystery of faith'. The Gospel accounts do not enter into these theological discussions. It was St Thomas Aquinas who first gave the interpretation used by the Catholic Church.

The overall teaching in John 6:25-59 remains more general. Jesus declares, 'I am the bread of life' (verses 35 & 48). Jesus contrasts the manna that God provided for the Israelites in the wilderness – which met their physical needs – with faith in the Son of Man, which meets their spiritual need for salvation. Jesus refers several times to 'coming down from heaven' (verses 38, 41, 51, 58) to show his message has its origin with God, who lives in heaven.

Verse 40 sums up God's heart in this teaching: 'For what my Father wants is that all who see the Son and believe in him should have eternal life.'

 # MEDITATIO:

- Reflect on the significance of Jesus describing himself as the bread of life.
- Is Jesus *your* bread of life? What practical difference does this make to you?
- How important is celebrating the Eucharist or Holy Communion in your Christian life?

 # ORATIO:

Humbly come before God in prayer. Give thanks to God for sending his Son as 'the bread of life' so that we can live in fellowship with the Trinity and, through faith in Jesus, inherit eternal life. Marvel at this wonderful gift.

 # CONTEMPLATIO:

'While they were eating, Jesus took a piece of bread,
gave a prayer of thanks, broke it, and gave it to his disciples.
"Take and eat it," he said; "this is my body."
Then he took a cup, gave thanks to God, and gave it to them.
"Drink it, all of you," he said; "this is my blood,
which seals God's covenant, my blood poured out for many
for the forgiveness of sins.' Matthew 26:26-28

Take time each day this week to give thanks that Jesus' death paid the price so you can receive forgiveness.

YOKED WITH JESUS

Matthew 11:25-30

[25] At that time Jesus said, "Father, Lord of heaven and earth! I thank you because you have shown to the unlearned what you have hidden from the wise and learned. [26] Yes, Father, this was how you wanted it to happen.

[27] "My Father has given me all things. No one knows the Son except the Father, and no one knows the Father except the Son and those to whom the Son chooses to reveal him.

[28] "Come to me, all of you who are tired from carrying heavy loads, and I will give you rest. [29] Take my yoke and put it on you, and learn from me, because I am gentle and humble in spirit; and you will find rest. [30] For the yoke I will give you is easy, and the load I will put on you is light."

Other Readings: Zechariah 9:9-10; Psalm 145:1-2, 8-11, 13-14; Romans 8:9, 11-13

 LECTIO:

Short as it is, this passage contains three separate parts: verses 25-26, 27 and 28-30. No one knows for sure but it is likely that Matthew brought these words of Jesus together in one place to highlight a single idea. He wanted us to see Jesus' deep relationship with God the Father and with believers.

The first part (verses 25-26) is Jesus' prayer of thanksgiving to his Father, 'Lord of heaven and earth'. The phrase 'heaven and earth' is used to encapsulate the whole of creation. So God's lordship is absolute and extends throughout the whole universe.

This description of God serves Jesus' purpose very neatly. It comes soon after he has spoken about the sceptics who refuse to believe in him or his ministry (verses 20-24). He says they cannot lift themselves up to heaven. In other words, people can only enter heaven by believing in him.

Belief in God is a gift revealed by God himself. It is not based on our education or our ability to learn. Unlearned people can believe in God while people the world considers wise or clever can be completely ignorant about God.

The next verse expresses the unique relationship between God the Father and God the Son, Jesus. Each knows the other completely. The Father has given all things to Jesus. In the first section it was the Father who revealed things. In this section it is Jesus who is revealing the Father. Jesus declares that knowledge of the Father depends entirely on the Son. Jesus chooses who shares this knowledge; it is his gift to give. And no one can pretend to have this knowledge without Jesus' help to understand or know the Father.

In the third section (verses 28-30) Jesus invites all who 'are tired from carrying heavy loads' to come to him because he offers rest. He invites them to put on his yoke.

The yoke represents the teaching a teacher gives to his students. Physical yokes were of course used to ensure that two animals worked together under the direction of the master. The image conveys that Jesus is in charge and his disciples need to follow his instructions. But Jesus promises he will lead us gently and humbly and the load will be light.

 MEDITATIO:

- Which things strike you most from these verses?
- Have you accepted the 'yoke' of following Jesus? Do you find this yoke easy and light?
- Have you found rest in following Jesus?
- What examples can you think of that demonstrate the gentleness and humility of Jesus?
- Consider the awesome power of God – Lord of heaven and earth. How do you respond to this?

 ORATIO:

Use the words of Psalm 145 to thank and praise God for his compassion, mercy and faithfulness.

You may have gained insight into the Father through your meditation. But perhaps you also see an area where you would like to understand more. Ask God to help you understand and give you the grace to draw closer to him.

 CONTEMPLATIO:

'But you do not live as your human nature tells you to;
instead you live as the Spirit tells you to...' Romans 8:9

If we follow Jesus he gives us the Holy Spirit to help us live in obedience to Jesus' yoke. Meditate further on Matthew 11:27-30. Let the words sink into your heart and ask the Holy Spirit to speak to you and guide you.

BEARING FRUIT

Matthew 13:1-9, 18-23*

¹ That same day Jesus left the house and went to the lakeside, where he sat down to teach. ² The crowd that gathered round him was so large that he got into a boat and sat in it, while the crowd stood on the shore. ³ He used parables to tell them many things.

"Once there was a man who went out to sow corn. ⁴ As he scattered the seed in the field, some of it fell along the path, and the birds came and ate it up. ⁵ Some of it fell on rocky ground, where there was little soil. The seeds soon sprouted, because the soil wasn't deep. ⁶ But when the sun came up, it burnt the young plants; and because the roots had not grown deep enough, the plants soon dried up. ⁷ Some of the seed fell among thorn bushes, which grew up and choked the plants. ⁸ But some seeds fell in good soil, and the plants produced corn; some produced a hundred grains, others sixty, and others thirty."

⁹ And Jesus concluded, "Listen, then, if you have ears!"

¹⁸ "Listen, then, and learn what the parable of the sower means. ¹⁹ Those who hear the message about the Kingdom but do not understand it are like the seeds that fell along the path. The Evil One comes and snatches away what was sown in them. ²⁰ The seeds that fell on rocky ground stand for those who receive the message gladly as soon as they hear it. ²¹ But it does not sink deep into them, and they don't last long. So when trouble or persecution comes because of the message, they give up at once. ²² The seeds that fell among thorn bushes stand for those who hear the message; but the worries about this life and the love for riches choke the message, and they don't bear fruit. ²³ And the seeds sown in the good soil stand for those who hear the message and understand it: they bear fruit, some as much as a hundred, others sixty, and others thirty."

*This is a shortened form of today's reading. The full reading is Matthew 13:1-23.

Other Readings: Isaiah 55:10-11; Psalm 65:9-13; Romans 8:18-23

 ## LECTIO:

Jesus frequently used parables, or simple short stories, to teach very profound truths about God. He based his parables around ordinary human experiences and used items familiar to most people. His parables normally had a simple plot and a single message.

In our text, Jesus paints a vivid word picture of the sower and the seeds. Each situation described in this parable has a specific meaning. The parable is about how various people receive the word of God and the harvest that results.

Jesus likens people to four different soil types. Three out of the four groups of people Jesus identifies don't allow God's word to produce the fruit that God intends. The reasons vary but the ultimate result is the same. Although they receive the message, they don't let it take root in them.

Only one group of people, 'the good soil', is fruitful. Different people produce various amounts of fruit but this group are all fruitful.

The responsibility of the sower is to sow the seed. The sower doesn't know what the potential harvest will be; only God knows that.

 ## MEDITATIO:

- How do you respond to God's word? Which of the four soil types do you feel describes you best? How do you feel about this?
- 'The seeds that fell in good soil stand for those who hear the message and retain it in a good and obedient heart, and they persist until they bear fruit.' (Luke 8:15). Does Luke's description of the 'good soil' help us understand this passage better? What can we learn from this verse?
- Consider how you might bear more fruit in your life.

 ## ORATIO:

Reflect on the scripture and respond to God humbly in prayer. Ask God to give you boldness and show you specific opportunities to share your faith.

 ## CONTEMPLATIO:

The ministry of your priest or pastor comes to you at their great personal cost. How has their ministry influenced you? What have you ignored or rejected that may be reducing the fruit you might bear? What can change in your attitude to their ministry over the coming weeks and months?

THE FINAL HARVEST

Matthew 13:24-30, 36-43*

²⁴ Jesus told them another parable: "The Kingdom of heaven is like this. A man sowed good seed in his field. ²⁵ One night, when everyone was asleep, an enemy came and sowed weeds among the wheat and went away. ²⁶ When the plants grew and the ears of corn began to form, then the weeds showed up. ²⁷ The man's servants came to him and said, 'Sir, it was good seed you sowed in your field; where did the weeds come from?' ²⁸ 'It was some enemy who did this,' he answered. 'Do you want us to go and pull up the weeds?' they asked him. ²⁹ 'No,' he answered, 'because as you gather the weeds you might pull up some of the wheat along with them. ³⁰ Let the wheat and the weeds both grow together until harvest. Then I will tell the harvest workers to pull up the weeds first, tie them in bundles and burn them, and then to gather in the wheat and put it in my barn.' "

³⁶ When Jesus had left the crowd and gone indoors, his disciples came to him and said, "Tell us what the parable about the weeds in the field means."

³⁷ Jesus answered, "The man who sowed the good seed is the Son of Man; ³⁸ the field is the world; the good seed is the people who belong to the Kingdom; the weeds are the people who belong to the Evil One; ³⁹ and the enemy who sowed the weeds is the Devil. The harvest is the end of the age, and the harvest workers are angels. ⁴⁰ Just as the weeds are gathered up and burnt in the fire, so the same thing will happen at the end of the age: ⁴¹ the Son of Man will send out his angels to gather up out of his Kingdom all those who cause people to sin and all others who do evil things, ⁴² and they will throw them into the fiery furnace, where they will cry and grind their teeth. ⁴³ Then God's people will shine like the sun in their Father's Kingdom. Listen, then, if you have ears!

This is a shortened form of today's reading. The full reading is Matthew 13:24-43.

Other Readings: Wisdom 12:13, 16-19; Psalm 86:5-6, 9-10, 15-16; Romans 8:26-27

 LECTIO:

Jesus' interpretation of this parable is important. The seeds here are not the 'word of God' as they were in the last parable about the sower (Matthew 13:1-9). Here Jesus is discussing the Church community, God's people in the world, although outwardly the two parables appear similar.

Those people who try to live as Jesus directs, he calls 'the people who belong to the kingdom'. Hidden in their midst are 'people who belong to the Evil One'. In other words, people who are not obeying God but whose lives are being directed the Devil.

The servants want to root out the weeds immediately but the master tells them to wait until harvest time. Similarly, in the church we should avoid judging each other. Judgement belongs to 'the Son of Man'; he is the only one who knows one seed from another.

In the meantime, the good seeds have until harvest time to grow and flourish even though the 'weeds' may hinder the harvest. Jesus refuses to intervene until harvest time; that is the end days.

There's a warning here for those who are churchgoers but not actually following Jesus. Each of us is to be alert and live our lives in obedience to Jesus. Everyone will have to give an account for their lives on judgement day.

 # MEDITATIO:

- What relevance does this parable have to your spiritual life?
- What can you learn from Jesus' teaching here?
- What is your response?

 # ORATIO:

> 'In the same way the Spirit also comes to help us, weak as we are.
> For we do not know how we ought to pray;
> the Spirit himself pleads with God for us in groans
> that words cannot express.' Romans 8:26

We all need God's help to follow him and this verse encourages us that the Holy Spirit is interceding for us. Respond to God in prayer. You may wish to pray, 'Lord give me the grace to hear your voice calling me to a deeper life of faith'.

 # CONTEMPLATIO:

Read Psalm 86 and meditate on the greatness and mercy of God.

KINGDOM TREASURE

Matthew 13:44-52

[44] "The Kingdom of heaven is like this. A man happens to find a treasure hidden in a field. He covers it up again, and is so happy that he goes and sells everything he has, and then goes back and buys that field.

[45] "Also, the Kingdom of heaven is like this. A man is looking for fine pearls, [46] and when he finds one that is unusually fine, he goes and sells everything he has, and buys that pearl.

[47] "Also, the Kingdom of heaven is like this. Some fishermen throw their net out in the lake and catch all kinds of fish. [48] When the net is full, they pull it to shore and sit down to divide the fish: the good ones go into their buckets, the worthless ones are thrown away. [49] It will be like this at the end of the age: the angels will go out and gather up the evil people from among the good [50] and will throw them into the fiery furnace, where they will cry and grind their teeth.

[51] "Do you understand these things?" Jesus asked them.

"Yes," they answered.

[52] So he replied, "This means, then, that every teacher of the Law who becomes a disciple in the Kingdom of heaven is like the owner of a house who takes new and old things out of his storeroom."

Other Readings: 1 Kings 3:5, 7-12; Psalm 119:57, 72, 76-77, 127-130;
Romans 8:28-30

 LECTIO:

Matthew 13 concludes with three more parables about the kingdom of heaven. The first two underline the value of following Jesus. It is so important and precious it is worth giving up everything else or 'selling all' to enter Jesus' new way of life.

As the parables suggest sometimes those who are not looking find the treasure; on other occasions those who have searched long and hard for their life's dream eventually find it.

The third parable tells us that our decision about following Jesus has serious consequences. God decides who has lived in obedience to the gospel and who has not. God alone is able to differentiate between individuals.

As Christians we face daily challenges to choose to live in obedience to Jesus. Sometimes we will fail but then we can seek God's forgiveness. We can be confident that, while it will certainly not always be easy, living God's way will always be worth the sacrifice.

Jesus ends this passage by referring to 'new and old things'. Jesus insists that he hasn't come to replace the Law of Moses and the teaching of the prophets but to fulfil them (Matthew 5:17). So the old treasures of the Law are given fresh meaning in the kingdom of heaven.

MEDITATIO:

- Who or what are the most precious treasures in your life? Where does Jesus appear on this list?
- What difficult decisions have you had to make to be a faithful Christian?
- What have you surrendered in order to follow Jesus?
- How much value do you place on your relationship with Jesus?

ORATIO:

Read the verses selected from Psalm 119. Can you echo these as a prayer?

In our reading from 1 Kings 3, Solomon asks God for wisdom. Take time to lay some of the challenges you face before God. Ask for his help and wisdom in dealing with them.

CONTEMPLATIO:

'We know that in all things God works for good with those who love him, those whom he has called according to his purpose. And so those whom God set apart, he called; and those he called, he put right with himself, and he shared his glory with them.' Romans 8: 28, 30

We face choices every day. What helps you to make these decisions? What part do the Bible and prayer play in your decision-making? How do you decide what God is saying to you personally? Let these words from Romans encourage you in the coming week.

YOU GIVE THEM SOMETHING

Matthew 14:13-21

[13] When Jesus heard the news about John, he left there in a boat and went to a lonely place by himself. The people heard about it, so they left their towns and followed him by land. [14] Jesus got out of the boat, and when he saw the large crowd, his heart was filled with pity for them, and he healed those who were ill.

[15] That evening his disciples came to him and said, "It is already very late, and this is a lonely place. Send the people away and let them go to the villages to buy food for themselves."

[16] "They don't have to leave," answered Jesus. "You yourselves give them something to eat!"

[17] "All we have here are five loaves and two fish," they replied.

[18] "Then bring them here to me," Jesus said. [19] He ordered the people to sit down on the grass; then he took the five loaves and the two fish, looked up to heaven, and gave thanks to God. He broke the loaves and gave them to the disciples, and the disciples gave them to the people. [20] Everyone ate and had enough. Then the disciples took up twelve baskets full of what was left over. [21] The number of men who ate was about 5,000, not counting the women and children.

Other Readings: Isaiah 55:1-3; Psalm 145:8-9, 15-18; Romans 8:35, 37-39

 LECTIO:

Our text today comes immediately after the martyrdom of John the Baptist (Matthew 14:1-12). Herod makes a rash promise at his birthday party which gives his lover, Herodias, the opportunity to silence John once and for all. John had been imprisoned for openly denouncing the adulterous relationship between Herod and his brother's wife. (Jewish Law expressly forbade a man to marry his brother's wife while the brother was still living, Leviticus 18:16, 20:21.)

The death of his cousin John saddened Jesus deeply. Quite understandably, he wants to be alone for a while so he takes a boat to a remote place across the lake. But the crowds can't leave him alone. They follow him to receive more healing miracles and hear his powerful teaching.

Matthew highlights Jesus' grief and his compassion for the people who search so hard for him. He looks into the hearts of the crowds and he doesn't ignore them (verse 14).

Later in the evening the disciples realise that people will be getting hungry, but in this remote place there is nowhere for them to buy food. So they suggest Jesus sends them off to the nearest villages. Jesus' reply must have stunned them, 'You yourselves give them something to eat!'

What is Jesus thinking? They don't even have enough food for themselves. How can they possibly feed all these people? It's impossible.

Jesus takes the loaves and fishes, gives thanks to God, breaks the bread and then the miracle takes place – the food just keeps on coming. Enough to feed 5,000 men plus women and children, and with twelve baskets left over!

Only this miracle is recorded by all four gospel writers. Matthew certainly intends us to see the parallel with God providing his people with manna in the wilderness under the leadership of Moses – but now one greater than Moses is here.

MEDITATIO:

- Imagine that you were an eyewitness to this miracle, firstly as one of the crowd, then as one of the disciples. What impact would it have had on you? How would you have reacted?
- What lessons can we learn from this miracle today? Are we compassionate? Should we be more open to the possibility of God intervening in situations miraculously to demonstrate his glory?
- Have you experienced a situation where you didn't have the ability or resources to meet a need but God intervened?

ORATIO:

Psalm 145:8-18 reminds us of God's compassion and enduring love. It also tells us that God is close to those who call to him from their hearts. What is the prayer of your heart? For what do you hunger? Take time to offer this hunger to God. And let the words of the psalm bring you comfort as you pray.

CONTEMPLATIO:

'You yourselves give them something to eat!'

Open your heart to God and spend some time meditating on what this phrase might mean for you. God may reveal something very specific over the coming days or weeks.

WHY DOUBT?

Matthew 14:22-33

²² Then Jesus made the disciples get into the boat and go on ahead to the other side of the lake, while he sent the people away. ²³ After sending the people away, he went up a hill by himself to pray. When evening came, Jesus was there alone; ²⁴ and by this time the boat was far out in the lake, tossed about by the waves, because the wind was blowing against it.

²⁵ Between three and six o'clock in the morning Jesus came to the disciples, walking on the water. ²⁶ When they saw him walking on the water, they were terrified. "It's a ghost!" they said, and screamed with fear.

²⁷ Jesus spoke to them at once. "Courage!" he said. "It is I. Don't be afraid!"

²⁸ Then Peter spoke up. "Lord, if it is really you, order me to come out on the water to you."

²⁹ "Come!" answered Jesus. So Peter got out of the boat and started walking on the water to Jesus. ³⁰ But when he noticed the strong wind, he was afraid and started to sink down in the water. "Save me, Lord!" he cried.

³¹ At once Jesus reached out and grabbed hold of him and said, "How little faith you have! Why did you doubt?"

³² They both got into the boat, and the wind died down. ³³ Then the disciples in the boat worshipped Jesus. "Truly you are the Son of God!" they exclaimed.

Other Readings: 1 Kings 19:9, 11-13; Psalm 85:8-13; Romans 9:1-5

 LECTIO:

At last Jesus is able to spend some time alone with his Father. Chapter 14 opened with the account of his cousin John the Baptist's murder. Jesus tried to be alone then but the crowds followed him. Jesus took pity on the people, taught them long into the evening, healed the sick and miraculously provided food for over 5,000 people.

Then he sends the disciples ahead of him in the boat across the lake and sends the people back home. Now he can grieve for John and pray to his Father. Prayer was the foundation of his life and ministry so he always made time for fellowship with his Father.

But the main theme of this passage is faith. Earlier that day the disciples had seen Jesus heal people and supernaturally transform five loaves and two fish into enough food for over 5,000 people with plenty to spare! Now Jesus comes walking on the water towards their boat. They can't believe their eyes. They are terrified and think they must be seeing a ghost. Jesus reassures them that it really is him so they don't need to be afraid.

As usual, Peter plunges in and literally takes a huge step of faith. Here again he probably speaks without thinking and asks Jesus to let him walk on water too. Jesus calls him. Peter steps out of the boat and starts walking on the water towards Jesus. Then he notices how stormy it is, fear floods in and he begins to sink. Jesus saves him and gently chides him, asking where his faith has gone.

The storm becomes calm. For the disciples this is now a time of worship and they exclaim 'Truly you are the Son of God!'

 MEDITATIO:

- What lessons about faith can we learn from this passage?
- Have you been in a situation when you called out to God for help? What happened?
- We can so easily start stepping out boldly in faith but then become afraid. How can we try to prevent doubt robbing us of what God wants for us?

 ORATIO:

Give thanks that Jesus truly is the Son of God and praise him for his power and compassion.

Opportunities to grow in faith are all around us. Ask Jesus to help you 'step out of the boat' in an area where you feel he is challenging you. Let the love of Jesus fill you and wash away fears from your heart.

 CONTEMPLATIO:

Jesus asks Peter a very revealing question, 'Why did you doubt?' Consider the reasons Peter had to doubt. Then consider that Jesus, the Son of God, was right there with him. Reflect on why you have doubts sometimes. If Jesus is with us how should this affect our faith?

PROMISE KEEPER

Luke 1:39-56

[39] Soon afterwards Mary got ready and hurried off to a town in the hill country of Judea. [40] She went into Zechariah's house and greeted Elizabeth. [41] When Elizabeth heard Mary's greeting, the baby moved within her. Elizabeth was filled with the Holy Spirit [42] and said in a loud voice, "You are the most blessed of all women, and blessed is the child you will bear! [43] Why should this great thing happen to me, that my Lord's mother comes to visit me? [44] For as soon as I heard your greeting, the baby within me jumped with gladness. [45] How happy you are to believe that the Lord's message to you will come true!"

[46] Mary said,

"My heart praises the Lord;
[47] my soul is glad because of God my Saviour,
[48] for he has remembered me, his lowly servant!
From now on all people will call me happy,
[49] because of the great things the Mighty God has done for me.
His name is holy;
[50] from one generation to another
he shows mercy to those who honour him.
[51] He has stretched out his mighty arm
and scattered the proud with all their plans.
[52] He has brought down mighty kings from their thrones,
and lifted up the lowly.
[53] He has filled the hungry with good things,
and sent the rich away with empty hands.
[54] He has kept the promise he made to our ancestors,
and has come to the help of his servant Israel.
[55] He has remembered to show mercy to Abraham
and to all his descendants for ever!"

[56] Mary stayed about three months with Elizabeth and then went back home.

*Other readings: Revelation 11:19, 12:1-6, 10; Psalm 45:9-11, 15;
1 Corinthians 15:20-26*

 LECTIO:

The Church has chosen this wonderful song of praise today to honour Jesus' mother Mary. In the preceding verses Mary has been told two remarkable things by the angel Gabriel (Luke 1:26-38). Firstly that Mary herself, although a virgin, will give birth to God's Son by the power of the Holy Spirit. Secondly, that her cousin Elizabeth, who has never been able to have children and is now very old, is six months' pregnant.

We begin with the meeting between the two expectant mothers. Mary knows that Elizabeth is pregnant, and when she sees her it must have been quite evident, but there is no record of Elizabeth having been told about Mary's news. In Luke's account Elizabeth confirms the angel Gabriel's promise to Mary by referring to her as 'my Lord's mother' under the inspiration of the Holy Spirit. The two women accept the incarnation as a matter of fact.

The simple faith and willingness of both Mary and Elizabeth to believe and embrace God's special plan for them and their babies shines through this passage. Both are aware that God is involved in their pregnancies and show extraordinary faith.

Mary responds with one of the great songs of praise in the Bible. She begins with personal thanks for 'the great things the Mighty God has done for me' (verse 49). Mary then extols the faithfulness and mercy of God in fulfilling his covenant promise to Abraham. There are echoes of Hannah's prayer in 1 Samuel 2:1-10 and the heartfelt cries of Old Testament messianic prophecies. Centuries of hope will very soon be fulfilled through the Saviour born to God's 'lowly servant'.

 ## MEDITATIO:

- What can we learn from both Mary and Elizabeth's response to God? What lessons can we apply in our own lives?
- What can we learn about faith and humility from this passage?
- What does this passage reveal about the nature and character of God?
- How can you serve Jesus?

 ## ORATIO:

Consider the 'great things' God has done for you. Make Mary's song of praise your own this week. Let the Holy Spirit speak to you from it and then respond to God in prayer. You might like to write your own psalm to magnify God and thank him for all he has done in your life.

 ## CONTEMPLATIO:

Reflect on Jesus your Saviour. What has he saved you from? What has he saved you for?

WHO DO YOU SAY I AM?

Matthew 16:13-20

[13] Jesus went to the territory near the town of Caesarea Philippi, where he asked his disciples, "Who do people say the Son of Man is?"

[14] "Some say John the Baptist," they answered. "Others say Elijah, while others say Jeremiah or some other prophet."

[15] "What about you?" he asked them. "Who do you say I am?"

[16] Simon Peter answered, "You are the Messiah, the Son of the living God."

[17] "Good for you, Simon son of John!" answered Jesus. "For this truth did not come to you from any human being, but it was given to you directly by my Father in heaven. [18] And so I tell you, Peter: you are a rock, and on this rock foundation I will build my church, and not even death will ever be able to overcome it. [19] I will give you the keys of the Kingdom of heaven; what you prohibit on earth will be prohibited in heaven, and what you permit on earth will be permitted in heaven."

[20] Then Jesus ordered his disciples not to tell anyone that he was the Messiah.

Other Readings: Isaiah 22:19-23; Psalm 138:1-3, 6, 8; Romans 11:33-36

 LECTIO:

In Jesus' day many Jews believed that God had promised to send them a Messiah or anointed king who would set Israel free from oppression and establish God's kingdom on earth. How this would work out in practice was unclear but a new king would certainly be a threat to Herod, the Roman authorities and ultimately to Caesar.

Jesus chooses a remote town, Caesarea Philippi in the far north-east of Israel, to discuss this revolutionary topic with his disciples. Jesus poses the question indirectly by asking who people say the 'Son of Man' is. The people think Jesus is a prophet of some kind, maybe John the Baptist, Elijah, or Jeremiah but they are not sure. So Jesus asks the disciples what they think.

Peter answers that Jesus is 'the Messiah, the Son of the living God'. Jesus commends Peter telling him that the Father has revealed this secret to him. In making this declaration Peter is proclaiming his allegiance to God's new anointed king. However it is important to note that the title 'Son of the Living God' was an Old Testament term that reinforced the term Messiah. When giving his reply Peter wouldn't have understood 'Son of God' in the divine sense or thought of Jesus as being part of the Trinity.

Jesus then declares that Peter will be the foundation stone for his new kingdom people, his church. This new community of people who are willing to declare their allegiance to God's appointed king starts right here with the disciples.

Jesus declares that death will not be able to overcome the members of this new community. Jesus also gives authority, or the keys of the kingdom of heaven, to the disciples. And finally, he insists they keep this revelation that he is the Messiah a secret for the time being.

 MEDITATIO:

- How would the disciples have felt after this revelation? Would it have changed the way they listened to Jesus? The mission had now become far more dangerous – Jesus was surely on a collision course with Herod and the Romans.
- Everyone has to answer Jesus' question, 'Who do you say that I am?' What is your response?
- Jesus chose Peter as the foundation for his Church in spite of his human failings. What can we learn from this?
- What do you think about the Church and the authority God has given it? Are you willing to accept authority? Do you exercise it in a godly way?

 ORATIO:

Ask God to give you an ever deeper knowledge and love for Jesus. Ask him to help you play your part in your church community.

 CONTEMPLATIO:

Reflect on these verses from Romans 11:33-36:

'How great are God's riches! How deep are his wisdom and knowledge! Who can explain his decisions? Who can understand his ways? As the scripture says,
"Who knows the mind of the Lord?
Who is able to give him advice?
Who has ever given him anything,
so that he had to pay it back?"
For all things were created by him, and all things exist through him and for him. To God be the glory for ever! Amen.'

FORGET YOURSELF

Matthew 16:21-27

²¹ From that time on Jesus began to say plainly to his disciples, "I must go to Jerusalem and suffer much from the elders, the chief priests, and the teachers of the Law. I will be put to death, but three days later I will be raised to life."

²² Peter took him aside and began to rebuke him. "God forbid it, Lord!" he said. "That must never happen to you!"

²³ Jesus turned around and said to Peter, "Get away from me, Satan! You are an obstacle in my way, because these thoughts of yours don't come from God, but from human nature."

²⁴ Then Jesus said to his disciples, "If anyone wants to come with me, he must forget self, carry his cross, and follow me. ²⁵ For whoever wants to save his own life will lose it; but whoever loses his life for my sake will find it. ²⁶ Will people gain anything if they win the whole world but lose their life? Of course not! There is nothing they can give to regain their life. ²⁷ For the Son of Man is about to come in the glory of his Father with his angels, and then he will reward each one according to his deeds.

Other Readings: Jeremiah 20:7-9; Psalm 63:1-5, 7-8; Romans 12:1-2

 LECTIO:

Having revealed to the disciples that he is the Messiah, Jesus stuns them by saying he is going to be put to death by the Jewish leaders in Jerusalem. This is the first of three occasions when Jesus speaks about this to his disciples (see Matthew 17:22-23, 20:17-19).

This makes no sense to the disciples. How could the Messiah, the centuries' old hope of Jewish deliverance be rejected and put to death by their own leaders? How could God allow it? What would be the point? Why would the Messiah suffer? Suffering in the minds of many Jews was still associated with sin and God's judgement.

Peter, having just been told he is the rock upon which the church will be built, temporarily becomes shifting sand. He voices his fear and frustration to Jesus, 'That must never happen to you'. Jesus replies with a strong rebuke echoing the dismissal he gave directly to Satan when he was tempted in the wilderness (Matthew 4:10). The strength of Jesus' rebuke indicates the seriousness of the temptation being placed before him.

Jesus may well have compounded the disciples' confusion by going on to talk about carrying crosses and losing your life to save it. We have the benefit of seeing things after the resurrection so Jesus' words carry the deep truth about laying down our own lives to live for him.

Jesus offers the disciples two glimmers of hope. First he tells them he will be raised from the dead (verse 21) and then he tells them that he will return in glory with the angels when he will judge people according to their deeds (verse 27).

 # MEDITATIO:

- The disciples must have been very confused by what Jesus tells them here but they don't give up. What can we learn from this?
- What do you think Jesus means when he says, 'whoever loses his life for my sake will find it?' What does this mean for you in your daily life?

 # ORATIO:

Give thanks that Jesus was prepared to do the will of his Father, even though this involved suffering and ultimately death.

Humbly come before God. Ask for his grace to help you to obey him day by day and live a life that pleases him rather than choosing your own comfort.

 # CONTEMPLATIO:

Meditate on these verses from Romans 12:1-2:

'So then, my brothers and sisters, because of God's great mercy to us I appeal to you: offer yourselves as a living sacrifice to God, dedicated to his service and pleasing to him. This is the true worship that you should offer. Do not conform yourselves to the standards of this world, but let God transform you inwardly by a complete change of your mind. Then you will be able to know the will of God – what is good and is pleasing to him and is perfect.'

BE RECONCILED

Matthew 18:15-20

[15] "If your brother sins against you, go to him and show him his fault. But do it privately, just between yourselves. If he listens to you, you have won your brother back. [16] But if he will not listen to you, take one or two other persons with you, so that 'every accusation may be upheld by the testimony of two or more witnesses,' as the scripture says. [17] And if he will not listen to them, then tell the whole thing to the church. Finally, if he will not listen to the church, treat him as though he were a pagan or a tax collector.

[18] "And so I tell all of you: what you prohibit on earth will be prohibited in heaven, and what you permit on earth will be permitted in heaven.

[19] "And I tell you more: whenever two of you on earth agree about anything you pray for, it will be done for you by my Father in heaven. [20] For where two or three come together in my name, I am there with them."

Other Readings: Ezekiel 33:7-9; Psalm 95:1-2, 6-9; Romans 13:8-10

 LECTIO:

Today's reading is part of what's known as Jesus' ecclesial teaching. The Greek word *ekklesia* is only used twice in the Gospels, here in verse 17 and two chapters earlier in Matthew 16:18.

The focus of Jesus' teaching here is on relationships between members of the local church community. He is fully aware of the human frailty of his disciples – and of us! There will be times when we are sinned against by our fellow Christians and we in turn will sin against them. So Jesus gives some practical instructions on how to deal with this.

The very first course of action is to try and sort it out one to one. If this works and your brother or sister sees their sin and repents then forgiveness can flow and the relationship is restored. No one else needs to be involved.

If this approach doesn't resolve the matter, Jesus instructs us to take along one or two others. He quotes from Deuteronomy 19:15 where God's instruction is that evidence needs to be established by more than just one witness. On a very practical level this adds a reality check to our own judgement of the situation so it is important that we choose people who can be objective.

If the person concerned still fails to repent then the matter needs to go the whole church, where a third opportunity is given for repentance. If this too is refused the person concerned can no longer be treated as a member of the church fellowship. Brotherly correction was a serious duty in the early church and still remains so today.

Jesus makes two amazing promises at the end of this passage, in verses 19 and 20. First he promises to be present with us if we come together in his name. Then he also promises that if two Christians agree about something in prayer God will not let their prayer go unanswered.

Through his living presence in the Christian community Jesus inspires our prayers and decisions. This is why dealing with divisions in the community is so important.

 # MEDITATIO:

- Why does Jesus place such importance on dealing with sin in the church community? Why is forgiveness a necessity?
- Do you find it easy to deal with conflict with other Christians? Or would you prefer to ignore it? Why is this harmful for both you and the other person concerned?
- Read Romans 13:8-10, part of which is given below. How do these verses relate to today's Gospel reading and our attitude towards people that sin against us?

  'Be under obligation to no one—the only obligation you have is to love one another. The commandments ... are summed up in the one command, "Love your neighbour as you love yourself." If you love others, you will never do them wrong;...'

 # ORATIO:

The Lord's Prayer reminds us that our personal forgiveness depends on our willingness to forgive those who sin against us. Pray for God's will to be done in your life and forgive anyone that has sinned against you.

 # CONTEMPLATIO:

In John 17:11 Jesus prays that his followers 'may be one just as you and I are one'. Think about the importance of unity in your local church community and the role of forgiveness in this.

DEBT FREE

Matthew 18:21-35

[21] Then Peter came to Jesus and asked, "Lord, if my brother keeps on sinning against me, how many times do I have to forgive him? Seven times?"

[22] "No, not seven times," answered Jesus, "but seventy times seven, [23] because the Kingdom of heaven is like this. Once there was a king who decided to check on his servants' accounts. [24] He had just begun to do so when one of them was brought in who owed him millions of pounds. [25] The servant did not have enough to pay his debt, so the king ordered him to be sold as a slave, with his wife and his children and all that he had, in order to pay the debt. [26] The servant fell on his knees before the king. 'Be patient with me,' he begged, 'and I will pay you everything!' [27] The king felt sorry for him, so he forgave him the debt and let him go.

[28] "Then the man went out and met one of his fellow-servants who owed him a few pounds. He grabbed him and started choking him. 'Pay back what you owe me!' he said. [29] His fellow-servant fell down and begged him, 'Be patient with me, and I will pay you back!' [30] But he refused; instead, he had him thrown into jail until he should pay the debt. [31] When the other servants saw what had happened, they were very upset and went to the king and told him everything. [32] So he called the servant in. 'You worthless slave!' he said. 'I forgave you the whole amount you owed me, just because you asked me to. [33] You should have had mercy on your fellow-servant, just as I had mercy on you.' [34] The king was very angry, and he sent the servant to jail to be punished until he should pay back the whole amount."

[35] And Jesus concluded, "That is how my Father in heaven will treat every one of you unless you forgive your brother from your heart."

Other Readings: Ecclesiasticus 27:30 – 28:7; Psalm 103:1-4, 9-12; Romans 14:7-9

 LECTIO:

We continue to look at Jesus' teaching on forgiveness. Peter wants to know how far forgiveness should stretch. So he asks how many times he must forgive a brother that keeps sinning against him. Is seven times enough? Jesus replies, 'seventy times seven'! It's not intended to be taken literally but rather to illustrate generosity of spirit. In effect Jesus is saying don't keep a record, just keep on forgiving.

Jesus adds a parable to illustrate his point. A servant owes the king a massive debt that he can never repay. He pleads for mercy and is completely released from the debt. The slate is wiped clean and he is given a fresh start. But the story doesn't end there. This servant is himself owed a small amount of money by a fellow-servant. Instead of showing him mercy too he does the opposite. He insists the debt is repaid in full and has him thrown into prison. The king is outraged when he learns of this behaviour, reinstates his debt and puts him in prison.

The message is clear. We are the servant that has been forgiven a massive debt we can never repay. If we fail to forgive someone a far smaller sin we will face God's judgement (verse 35).

As Christians we must be willing to forgive fellow Christians without delay when they sin against us. In this way we demonstrate God's love and forgiveness to the world. Without mutual forgiveness our church community has no credible witness.

 # MEDITATIO:

- What does this parable teach us about God's nature?
- Do you recognise that you have been forgiven a huge debt of sin you can never repay? How does this affect your willingness to forgive others?
- In this parable the king simply cancelled the debt but God couldn't deal with our sin like that. How was our debt paid? What is our response?

 # ORATIO:

Today most people ignore or excuse sin. How do you view your own sin? God calls us to be holy. Use Psalm 51 as a prayer and confess your sin to God who is rich in mercy.

 # CONTEMPLATIO:

Meditate on the wonderful promises of Psalm 103.

> 'As high as the sky is above the earth,
>   so great is his love for those who honour him.
> As far as the east is from the west,
>   so far does he remove our sins from us.'

TOO GENEROUS?

Matthew 20:1-16

[1] "The Kingdom of heaven is like this. Once there was a man who went out early in the morning to hire some men to work in his vineyard. [2] He agreed to pay them the regular wage, a silver coin a day, and sent them to work in his vineyard. [3] He went out again to the market place at nine o'clock and saw some men standing there doing nothing, [4] so he told them, 'You also go and work in the vineyard, and I will pay you a fair wage.' [5] So they went. Then at twelve o'clock and again at three o'clock he did the same thing. [6] It was nearly five o'clock when he went to the market place and saw some other men still standing there. 'Why are you wasting the whole day here doing nothing?' he asked them. [7] 'No one hired us,' they answered. 'Well, then, you also go and work in the vineyard,' he told them.

[8] "When evening came, the owner told his foreman, 'Call the workers and pay them their wages, starting with those who were hired last and ending with those who were hired first.' [9] The men who had begun to work at five o'clock were paid a silver coin each. [10] So when the men who were the first to be hired came to be paid, they thought they would get more; but they too were given a silver coin each. [11] They took their money and started grumbling against the employer. [12] 'These men who were hired last worked only one hour,' they said, 'while we put up with a whole day's work in the hot sun – yet you paid them the same as you paid us!'

[13] " 'Listen, friend,' the owner answered one of them, 'I have not cheated you. After all, you agreed to do a day's work for one silver coin. [14] Now take your pay and go home. I want to give this man who was hired last as much as I have given you. [15] Don't I have the right to do as I wish with my own money? Or are you jealous because I am generous?' "

[16] And Jesus concluded, "So those who are last will be first, and those who are first will be last."

Other Readings: Isaiah 55:6-9; Psalm 145:2-3, 8-9, 17-18; Philippians 1:20-24, 27

 LECTIO:

Jesus tells this parable to teach us something about God and his new kingdom. It's not intended as a comment about social justice.

As in other parables God is the owner and the vineyard his kingdom. At different times of the day he hires people to come and work in his vineyard. Perhaps the workers that were hired last were the ones no one else wanted. Surprisingly, when the wages are paid everyone gets the same. Those who toiled for 12 hours get exactly the same as those who only put in an hour right at the end.

The 'wage' or reward is really a covenant promise – eternal life in God's presence. It's not a reward for kingdom service but God's gift. God doesn't measure out his love and grace so some get more and others less. God lavishes his grace on whoever he chooses.

The truth is that everyone, including those who have had the privilege of serving God for a long time, gets more than they deserve.

 MEDITATIO:

- What does this parable teach us about our attitude to serving God, our pride and our attitude to our fellow Christians? Are we jealous of others?
- The owner hired workers that no one wanted. What can we learn from this?
- What does this parable teach us about God's character?

 ORATIO:

The owner sought out new workers several times during the day, underlining his urgency to see the harvest finished on time. Jesus urged his disciples to ask God to send more workers to bring in the harvest. Pray that the church will have enough workers for the mission. Ask what part you can play in sharing the gospel and nurturing disciples.

 CONTEMPLATIO:

Reflect on these verses from Isaiah 55:8-9:

> "'My thoughts,' says the Lord, "are not like yours,
>   and my ways are different from yours.
> As high as the heavens are above the earth,
>   so high are my ways and thoughts above yours."'

TRUE SERVANTS

Matthew 21:28-32

²⁸ "Now, what do you think? There was once a man who had two sons. He went to the elder one and said, 'Son, go and work in the vineyard today.' ²⁹ 'I don't want to,' he answered, but later he changed his mind and went. ³⁰ Then the father went to the other son and said the same thing. 'Yes, sir,' he answered, but he did not go. ³¹ Which one of the two did what his father wanted?"

"The elder one," they answered.

So Jesus said to them, "I tell you: the tax collectors and the prostitutes are going into the Kingdom of God ahead of you. ³² For John the Baptist came to you showing you the right path to take, and you would not believe him; but the tax collectors and the prostitutes believed him. Even when you saw this, you did not later change your minds and believe him.

Other Readings: Ezekiel 18:25-28; Psalm 25:4-9; Philippians 2:1-11

 LECTIO:

To help us understand this parable we need to look back to events earlier in the chapter. Matthew 21 opens with Jesus arriving in Jerusalem to a hero's welcome. Some people proclaim him to be 'David's Son', the long awaited Messiah. Jesus then causes chaos in the Temple, overturning tables, sending Temple money flying and driving away the people who were buying and selling.

Not surprisingly, the chief priests and elders want to know what authority he has to act in this way (verse 23). Jesus replies by asking them a loaded question about John the Baptist that leaves them floundering (verses 25-27).

Jesus then reinforces his point to the religious leaders by telling them this parable of the two sons. The father asks his elder son to work in his vineyard. This son begins by refusing but later has a change of heart and goes to work. The other son agrees initially but his actions don't match his words. He doesn't follow through. The religious leaders are led to conclude that it is the elder son that actually did what his father wanted.

Jesus then reveals that it is the prostitutes and tax collectors who are the elder son. While they initially rejected God's call to serve him, they have had a change of heart. They accepted John's message. They accept Jesus' teaching. They repent and start living the kingdom lifestyle.

The shocking conclusion is that the religious leaders are in fact behaving like the other son. They are maintaining the outward appearance of being religious but are failing to do God's will. They refuse to accept God's messengers. They rejected John the Baptist and now they are rejecting their own Messiah.

 MEDITATIO:

- This parable gives us the opportunity to review our relationship with God. If we initially said 'yes' to him, are we continuing to obey him? Are we merely keeping up an outward appearance of serving him but really just doing what we want?
- Consider how God wants you to serve him at this time in your life. How are you responding to his call?
- What can we learn from this parable about God's grace and our attitudes to others?

 ORATIO:

Make your own response to God. You may find these verses from Psalm 25:5, 9-10 a helpful prayer:

> 'Teach me to live according to your truth,
> for you are my God, who saves me.
> I always trust in you.
> He leads the humble in the right way
> and teaches them his will.
> With faithfulness and love he leads
> all who keep his covenant and obey his commands.'

 CONTEMPLATIO:

Read Philippians 2:1-11. Meditate on the wonderful description of Jesus' humility and greatness in verses 5-11. Now consider your response to Paul's exhortation,

> 'Don't do anything from selfish ambition or from a cheap desire to boast, but be humble toward one another, always considering others better than yourselves. And look out for one another's interests, not just for your own.'

PROPER FRUIT

Matthew 21:33-43

[33] "Listen to another parable," Jesus said. "There was once a landowner who planted a vineyard, put a fence around it, dug a hole for the winepress, and built a watchtower. Then he let out the vineyard to tenants and went on a journey. [34] When the time came to gather the grapes, he sent his slaves to the tenants to receive his share of the harvest. [35] The tenants seized his slaves, beat one, killed another, and stoned another. [36] Again the man sent other slaves, more than the first time, and the tenants treated them the same way. [37] Last of all he sent his son to them. 'Surely they will respect my son,' he said. [38] But when the tenants saw the son, they said to themselves, 'This is the owner's son. Come on, let's kill him, and we will get his property!' [39] So they seized him, threw him out of the vineyard, and killed him.

[40] "Now, when the owner of the vineyard comes, what will he do to those tenants?" Jesus asked.

[41] "He will certainly kill those evil men," they answered, "and let the vineyard out to other tenants, who will give him his share of the harvest at the right time."

[42] Jesus said to them, "Haven't you ever read what the Scriptures say?

'The stone which the builders rejected as worthless
    turned out to be the most important of all.
This was done by the Lord;
    what a wonderful sight it is!'

[43] "And so I tell you," added Jesus, "the Kingdom of God will be taken away from you and given to a people who will produce the proper fruits."

Other Readings: Isaiah 5:1-7; Psalm 80:8, 11-15, 18-19; Philippians 4:6-9

 ## LECTIO:

We are in the days between Jesus' triumphant entry into Jerusalem and his crucifixion. Jesus tells this parable while he is teaching in the temple.

The metaphor of God's people Israel being a vineyard would have been familiar to Jesus' listeners. The parallels with today's liturgy reading from Isaiah 5:1-7 are particularly striking. God lovingly plants the vineyard and expects it to bear fruit but all it produces is sour grapes. Isaiah was one of the many prophets God sent to warn the people to repent and return to God or face judgement.

Jesus makes the meaning of this parable even more explicit and makes some very significant additions.

The vineyard is entrusted to the care of tenants. When harvest time comes the owner sends his slaves to collect his share. The tenants take no notice of the slaves, beat some and kill others. Finally, the owner sends his son in the hope that they will at least show him respect. The tenants kill the son too, thinking they will now be able to claim the vineyard for themselves.

Before revealing the meaning of the parable Jesus asks the people what the owner should do with the tenants. Without realising that they are passing judgement on themselves, the people reply, 'let the vineyard out to other tenants' (verse 41).

Having got the people incensed at the tenants' behaviour, Jesus reveals the sting in the tail – they are the tenants (verse 43)! They will receive the sentence that they passed themselves. The vineyard (kingdom of God) will be given to 'a people who will produce the proper fruits'.

The most significant addition that Jesus makes is to identify himself as the owner's son. He does so indirectly by quoting from Psalm 118. This is another opportunity for the Jewish leaders to repent but they refuse and will go on to fulfil the parable literally by insisting that Jesus is put to death.

 MEDITATIO:

- This parable was told as a warning to the Jewish leaders but what lessons can we learn from it for our lives today?
- Consider the significance of Psalm 118:22-23. In rejecting Jesus the Jewish leaders rejected their most important prophet. They rejected God's Son and their Messiah and saviour. Are we in danger of rejecting Jesus' authority in our lives?
- What is the 'proper fruit' that Jesus expects from his followers today?
- What can we learn from Isaiah 5:7 about the sort of behaviour God expects from his people?

 ORATIO:

Respond to God in prayer. Ask God to show you how to live a life that bears more fruit for him.

 CONTEMPLATIO:

Meditate on Jesus the cornerstone, the most important stone of all. Is he the cornerstone of your life? Does he have the place of greatest honour?

WEDDING INVITATION

Matthew 22:1-14

[1] Jesus again used parables in talking to the people. [2] "The Kingdom of heaven is like this. Once there was a king who prepared a wedding feast for his son. [3] He sent his servants to tell the invited guests to come to the feast, but they did not want to come. [4] So he sent other servants with this message for the guests: 'My feast is ready now; my bullocks and prize calves have been butchered, and everything is ready. Come to the wedding feast!' [5] But the invited guests paid no attention and went about their business: one went to his farm, another to his shop, [6] while others grabbed the servants, beat them, and killed them. [7] The king was very angry; so he sent his soldiers, who killed those murderers and burnt down their city. [8] Then he called his servants and said to them, 'My wedding feast is ready, but the people I invited did not deserve it. [9] Now go to the main streets and invite to the feast as many people as you find.' [10] So the servants went out into the streets and gathered all the people they could find, good and bad alike; and the wedding hall was filled with people.

[11] "The king went in to look at the guests and saw a man who was not wearing wedding clothes. [12] 'Friend, how did you get in here without wedding clothes?' the king asked him. But the man said nothing. [13] Then the king told the servants, 'Tie him up hand and foot, and throw him outside in the dark. There he will cry and grind his teeth.' "

[14] And Jesus concluded, "Many are invited, but few are chosen."

Other Readings: Isaiah 25:6-10; Psalm 23; Philippians 4:12-14, 19-20

 LECTIO:

Jesus' listeners may well still be feeling battered by the parable of the wicked tenants but he continues to reinforce the point, telling this parable to explain what the Kingdom of heaven is like.

A king is preparing a wedding feast for his son. He sends his servants to tell the invited guests that everything is ready but the guests aren't interested. They add insult to injury by abusing the king's servants, even killing some of them. The king responds by burning down their city – probably an allusion to the destruction of Jerusalem in AD 70.

The king then instructs the servants to invite the 'good and the bad alike' straight off the streets. The king comes to meet the guests. He discovers one man who is not wearing wedding clothes and throws him out of the feast. Jesus concludes with the words, 'Many are invited, but few are chosen'.

Jesus doesn't provide an interpretation of the parable but clearly the king is God and his son is Jesus. The Jewish leaders and people are first on the invitation list. The way the king's servants are treated echoes the treatment of God's prophets and repeats the actions of the tenants in the earlier parable. The invitation is then thrown wide open. There are plenty of examples in the Gospels where those who are considered 'sinners' by the religious establishment become followers of Jesus. And now Gentiles as well as Jews are invited to the feast.

What are we to make of the guest not wearing wedding clothes? While 'good and bad alike' are invited God does not expect us to stay that way. We can only be in God's presence if we have received his holiness. If we reject God's invitation we have to face God's judgement and exclusion from his presence. The invitation is there. We both choose our response and are chosen by God.

 MEDITATIO:

- What is your response to Jesus' invitation? Are you willing to accept or are you too busy?
- Many people in Jesus' day, including those who considered themselves religious, were actually spiritually blind and deaf. They failed to see God at work in Jesus. How can we stay spiritually alert?
- What are the 'wedding clothes' Jesus expects us to wear?
- Why do you think Jesus uses the image of a wedding feast for this parable?

 ORATIO:

Use Psalm 23 as the basis for your prayers today.

 CONTEMPLATIO:

Meditate on the wonderful picture of salvation that Isaiah paints in Isaiah 25:6-10.

PAYING GOD

Matthew 22:15-21

[15] The Pharisees went off and made a plan to trap Jesus with questions. [16] Then they sent to him some of their disciples and some members of Herod's party. "Teacher," they said, "we know that you tell the truth. You teach the truth about God's will for people, without worrying about what others think, because you pay no attention to anyone's status. [17] Tell us, then, what do you think? Is it against our Law to pay taxes to the Roman Emperor, or not?"

[18] Jesus, however, was aware of their evil plan, and so he said, "You hypocrites! Why are you trying to trap me? [19] Show me the coin for paying the tax!"

They brought him the coin, [20] and he asked them, "Whose face and name are these?"

[21] "The Emperor's," they answered.

So Jesus said to them, "Well, then, pay the Emperor what belongs to the Emperor, and pay God what belongs to God."

Other Readings: Isaiah 45:1, 4-6; Psalm 96:1, 3-5, 7-10; 1 Thessalonians 1:1-5

 LECTIO:

The Pharisees have already been criticised by Jesus in the parables of the tenants and the wedding feast. Today's reading marks the first of four disputes between Jesus and the religious leaders.

The Pharisees have thought long and hard about how they might trap Jesus and they are confident that they have come up with the perfect question: 'is it against our Law to pay taxes to the Roman Emperor or not?'

This was one of the hottest issues of the day. The Romans had invaded and occupied their country and now taxed the Jews for the privilege! Paying taxes to the Romans was a symbol of defeat, subjugation and a source of bitter resentment. The very coin they had to use in paying the tax was another insult. The Jews were not allowed to put images of people on their coins but Caesar had his image stamped on his. It also carried the inscription 'son of the divine Augustus'. This would have been an affront to any devout Jew as only God was divine.

It appears to be a 'no win' situation for Jesus. Surely someone heralding God's new kingdom can't possibly endorse such an unjust tax. If he is their Messiah, delivering Israel from its oppressors must be top of his list. Jesus will be finished if he supports the tax and all his followers will desert him as a traitor, with their hopes dashed. If, on the other hand, he opposes the tax he will be openly inciting people to defy the Romans and will soon end up like every other revolutionary – hanging on a cross.

Jesus is fully aware of the trap. He asks them whose face and name are on the coin although he is fully aware of the answer. Then comes the masterful reply which doesn't give them enough to report him to the Romans but won't cause his followers to desert him either, 'pay to the Emperor what belongs to the Emperor, and pay God what belongs to God.'

We have to interpret this passage in the light of the whole story. Jesus' answer isn't intended as a comprehensive statement of the relationship between God and political authority. Jesus is not afraid of confrontation. He is fully aware that he is walking towards his death but it will be on his terms. He knows that ultimately the kingdom of God will defeat the Emperor's kingdom but it will do so on a far more fundamental level by defeating an even greater empire, death itself.

 # MEDITATIO:

- What do we learn about Jesus from this passage?
- Consider the irony and insincerity of the Pharisees words, 'we know that you tell the truth. You teach the truth about God's will for people' (verse 16).
- Do you worry about what others think of you? Do you treat people differently according to their social status?

 # ORATIO:

Read through Psalm 96 several times and let its words inspire you. Bring your offering of worship and praise to God.

 # CONTEMPLATIO:

Reflect on Jesus' instruction, 'pay God what belongs to God'. What does belong to God? Consider whether you are giving all you should to God. Ask the Holy Spirit to speak to you.

LOVE

Matthew 22:34-40

³⁴ When the Pharisees heard that Jesus had silenced the Sadducees, they came together, ³⁵ and one of them, a teacher of the Law, tried to trap him with a question. ³⁶ "Teacher," he asked, "which is the greatest commandment in the Law?"

³⁷ Jesus answered, " 'Love the Lord your God with all your heart, with all your soul, and with all your mind.' ³⁸ This is the greatest and the most important commandment. ³⁹ The second most important commandment is like it: 'Love your neighbour as you love yourself.' ⁴⁰ The whole Law of Moses and the teachings of the prophets depend on these two commandments."

Other Readings: Exodus 22:20-26; Psalm 18:1-3, 46, 50; 1 Thessalonians 1:5-10

 LECTIO:

In Matthew's account this is the third dispute with the religious leaders. Last week we saw how Jesus comprehensively outmanoeuvred the Pharisees on the question of paying taxes to Rome. Immediately before this reading the Sadducees were put right on the issue of bodily resurrection. In today's passage the Pharisees make another attempt to discredit Jesus' teaching publicly.

Many Jewish teachers debated which was the greatest out of all the 613 commandments in the Law of Moses. It is clear that they hope to trap Jesus with this question. Perhaps they hope he might dismiss the Law of Moses completely or give an answer they can ridicule. By now they should know better.

Jesus' initial answer would have been accepted by most Pharisees as he quotes from Deuteronomy 6:5, 'Love the Lord your God with all your heart, with all your soul, and with all your mind.' This was the foundation of the Jewish faith, *Shema* Israel, a daily prayer and reminder of allegiance to the one true living God.

Jesus then links this to Leviticus 19:18, 'Love your neighbour as you love yourself'. Love then is at the centre of the greatest commandment. Firstly love for God which then overflows into our relationships with people around us. The two must go hand in hand. As John expresses it so directly in his first letter (1 John 4:20), 'If we say we love God, but hate our brothers and sisters, we are liars. For people cannot love God, whom they have not seen, if they do not love their brothers and sisters, whom they have seen.'

We mustn't forget the context of today's reading. Jesus is living his last few days on earth before his death. Matthew wants us to see that in submitting to crucifixion Jesus is fulfilling both these commands: loving God through obedience to his will and loving his brothers and sisters by being separated from his father in order to restore us to fellowship with God.

Lastly, if we think back to the Sermon on the Mount Jesus' new kingdom lifestyle is about an invitation and promise for a new way of living with the help of the Holy Spirit rather than struggling to obey commandments in our own strength. Those who fully grasp and embrace Jesus' kingdom lifestyle will be blessed indeed.

 # MEDITATIO:

- Think about the example Jesus gives us in fulfilling these commandments in the way he lived his life on earth.
- Mark describes a similar encounter in Mark 12:28-34. There the question is asked genuinely and the teacher of the law draws the conclusion that obeying these commandments is more important than offering animal sacrifices, the central feature of worship at the time. Can we fall into the trap of thinking more about observing religious practices and miss what God wants from us the most?
- Read Exodus 22:20-26. These verses provide some practical examples of loving our neighbour. Think about the opportunities you have to show God's love to people around you.

 # ORATIO:

Humbly come before God and ask the Holy Spirit to help you love God with all your heart, soul and mind. Ask him to reveal God to you in a deeper way and remind you of things you may have forgotten. Let God minister his love to you.

When you feel ready, ask God to speak to you about loving your neighbour.

 # CONTEMPLATIO:

Reminding ourselves of God's character is a good way to renew our love for him. Take time to read through the whole of Psalm 18 over the next week.

HUMBLE YOURSELF

Matthew 23:1-12

¹ Then Jesus spoke to the crowds and to his disciples. ² "The teachers of the Law and the Pharisees are the authorized interpreters of Moses' Law. ³ So you must obey and follow everything they tell you to do; do not, however, imitate their actions, because they don't practise what they preach. ⁴ They tie on to people's backs loads that are heavy and hard to carry, yet they aren't willing even to lift a finger to help them carry those loads. ⁵ They do everything so that people will see them. Look at the straps with scripture verses on them which they wear on their foreheads and arms, and notice how large they are! Notice also how long are the tassels on their cloaks! ⁶ They love the best places at feasts and the reserved seats in the synagogues; ⁷ they love to be greeted with respect in the market places and to be called 'Teacher'. ⁸ You must not be called 'Teacher', because you are all members of one family and have only one Teacher. ⁹ And you must not call anyone here on earth 'Father', because you have only the one Father in heaven. ¹⁰ Nor should you be called 'Leader', because your one and only leader is the Messiah. ¹¹ The greatest one among you must be your servant. ¹² Whoever makes himself great will be humbled, and whoever humbles himself will be made great.

Other Readings: Malachi 1:14 – 2:2, 8-10; Psalm 131; 1 Thessalonians 2:7-9, 13

 LECTIO:

Matthew wrote his gospel account after Mark and he includes practically all of Mark's material. But he also includes a lot more of Jesus' teaching. This is organised in five main blocks, starting with the Sermon on the Mount in chapters 5-7. The commissioning of the disciples follows in chapter 10, the parables of the kingdom in chapter 13 and teaching about living as God's new kingdom community in chapter 18. Today's reading comes just before the final section, chapters 24-25, looking to the second coming and final judgement.

A substantial part of this teaching involves Jesus' denunciation of Israel's religious leaders. Jesus accuses them of being hypocrites. While they are indeed experts in the Law of Moses they are not practising what they preach. This incenses Jesus because they are burdening the people with a heavy load but they aren't willing 'to lift a finger to help' (verse 4) or to carry this burden themselves. This is in direct contrast to Jesus, who offers a light load and an easy yoke (Matthew 11:30).

Before and after this passage we learn that the leaders' sins are compounded by the fact that they are neglecting the really important teachings of the law, the greatest commandments (Matthew 22:37-39), and justice, mercy and honesty (Matthew 23:23).

So while Jesus instructs the people to follow the law he warns them not to imitate the lifestyle of their religious leaders. Instead of serving God and the people the leaders had become self-serving, full of pride and absorbed with their own importance and position in society.

Servanthood and humility, as demonstrated when Jesus washes the disciple's feet (John 13), is the pattern for Jesus' kingdom community. As Christians we should look to Jesus as our teacher, our leader, our Messiah. And we should look to God as our heavenly Father. Greatness in God's kingdom is to be found in humble service.

 ## MEDITATIO:

- If you are not a leader in your church community it can be easy to think that this passage doesn't apply to you. But it has much to say about the attitude and behaviour of 'ordinary' Christians too. Take some time to think these through.
- How can you cultivate the humble attitude of a servant?
- What kind of leaders does Jesus expect for his church?

 ## ORATIO:

Leaders in the church carry a heavy responsibility before God for the spiritual oversight of God's people. Pray for your leaders. Ask God to protect and equip them. Ask God to help you deal with areas of pride in your own life.

 ## CONTEMPLATIO:

Reflect on these verses from Psalm 131:

> 'Lord, I have given up my pride
> and turned away from my arrogance.
> I am not concerned with great matters
> or with subjects too difficult for me.
> Instead, I am content and at peace.
> As a child lies quietly in its mother's arms,
> so my heart is quiet within me.
> Israel, trust in the Lord
> now and forever!'

BE WISE

Matthew 25:1-13

¹ "At that time the Kingdom of heaven will be like this. Once there were ten young women who took their oil lamps and went out to meet the bridegroom. ² Five of them were foolish, and the other five were wise. ³ The foolish ones took their lamps but did not take any extra oil with them, ⁴ while the wise ones took containers full of oil for their lamps. ⁵ The bridegroom was late in coming, so the women began to nod and fall asleep.

⁶ "It was already midnight when the cry rang out, 'Here is the bridegroom! Come and meet him!' ⁷ The ten women woke up and trimmed their lamps. ⁸ Then the foolish ones said to the wise ones, 'Let us have some of your oil, because our lamps are going out.' ⁹ 'No, indeed,' the wise ones answered, 'there is not enough for you and for us. Go to the shop and buy some for yourselves.' ¹⁰ So the foolish women went off to buy some oil; and while they were gone, the bridegroom arrived. The five who were ready went in with him to the wedding feast, and the door was closed.

¹¹ "Later the other women arrived. 'Sir, sir! Let us in!' they cried out. ¹² 'Certainly not! I don't know you,' the bridegroom answered."

¹³ And Jesus concluded, "Be on your guard, then, because you do not know the day or the hour.

Other Readings: Wisdom 6:12-16; Psalm 63:1-7; 1 Thessalonians 4:13-18

 # LECTIO:

This passage is part of Jesus' 'eschatological' (end time) teaching in chapters 24-25. This parable marks the first of three about the coming of the Son of Man for final judgement. We will look at the others over the next two weeks.

Jesus probably intended this parable to be understood on two levels, referring both to his first and second coming.

One thing to note in this parable is that Jesus draws strongly on the Jewish tradition of contrasting wisdom and foolishness. The writer of Proverbs personifies these qualities as two women calling out to men and offering them their respective lifestyles. In this parable the five wise young women are the ones who have thought ahead and are prepared for the bridegroom. They are contrasted with the five foolish young women who, when the time comes, are not ready.

Jesus uses this parable to reinforce the importance of being alert and ready for his second coming. In the previous chapter (Matthew 24:36-44) Jesus teaches us to be ready for the unexpected. He will return, we can be certain of that. But no one knows when it will be, not even Jesus himself; only God the Father knows the exact time. For people living on earth at the time it will be 'when you are not expecting him' (verse 44).

This parable was also intended to speak directly to Jesus' fellow Jews. The central issue since his triumphant arrival in Jerusalem (Matthew 21:1-11) had been whether he was Israel's promised Messiah. Elsewhere in Matthew (9:15) Jesus refers to himself as the bridegroom and in an earlier parable (Matthew 22:1-14) he speaks about the guests refusing to come to the wedding feast prepared by the king in honour of his son. For centuries the people of Israel had longed for their Messiah. They were the invited guests. When the time comes and their Messiah is living among them some are ready while others, like the foolish young women, are unprepared.

 # MEDITATIO:

- In Matthew 7:24-27 Jesus contrasts two house builders. The wise one builds on rock, the foolish one builds on sand. One heard Jesus' teaching and obeyed it. The other also heard Jesus' teaching but didn't follow it. How does this help our understanding of the parable we are looking at today?
- Have you recognised Jesus as the Messiah who will return as judge?
- Are you living your life as a follower of Jesus? Does your lifestyle match what you say you believe?

 # ORATIO:

In 1 Thessalonians 4:13-18 Paul reminds us of the salvation hope we have in Jesus. Give thanks that through Jesus' death and resurrection we can be forgiven and reconciled to God. Ask the Holy Spirit to help you live each day in obedience to him.

 # CONTEMPLATIO:

Meditate on these verses from Proverbs 3:5-7:

'Trust in the Lord with all your heart. Never rely on what you think you know. Remember the Lord in everything you do, and he will show you the right way. Never let yourself think that you are wiser than you are; simply obey the Lord and refuse to do wrong.'

USE YOUR TALENTS

Matthew 25:14-19, 24-30*

¹⁴ "At that time the Kingdom of heaven will be like this. Once there was a man who was about to go on a journey; he called his servants and put them in charge of his property. ¹⁵ He gave to each one according to his ability: to one he gave five thousand gold coins, to another he gave two thousand, and to another he gave one thousand. Then he left on his journey. ¹⁶ The servant who had received five thousand coins went at once and invested his money and earned another five thousand. ¹⁷ In the same way the servant who had received two thousand coins earned another two thousand. ¹⁸ But the servant who had received one thousand coins went off, dug a hole in the ground, and hid his master's money.

¹⁹ "After a long time the master of those servants came back and settled accounts with them.

²⁴ "Then the servant who had received one thousand coins came in and said, 'Sir, I know you are a hard man; you reap harvests where you did not sow, and you gather crops where you did not scatter seed. ²⁵ I was afraid, so I went off and hid your money in the ground. Look! Here is what belongs to you.'

²⁶ " 'You bad and lazy servant!' his master said. 'You knew, did you, that I reap harvests where I did not sow, and gather crops where I did not scatter seed? ²⁷ Well, then, you should have deposited my money in the bank, and I would have received it all back with interest when I returned. ²⁸ Now, take the money away from him and give it to the one who has ten thousand coins. ²⁹ For to every person who has something, even more will be given, and he will have more than enough; but the person who has nothing, even the little that he has will be taken away from him. ³⁰ As for this useless servant – throw him outside in the darkness; there he will cry and grind his teeth.'

*For the full parable also read verses 20-23.

Other Readings: Proverbs 31:10-13, 19-20, 30-31; Psalm 128:1-5; 1 Thessalonians 5:1-6

 LECTIO:

On one level Jesus probably intended the religious leaders of his day to understand this parable as being directed against them. They behaved like the wicked servant, hiding God's truth rather than making it a light for the world

(Matthew 5:14-16) and locking the doors to the Kingdom of heaven rather than opening them (Matthew 23:13-14).

The parable also speaks to us today about being good stewards of the gifts and resources God has entrusted to us. The master is going away so he entrusts different amounts of his money to three servants according to their abilities (verse 15). It is important to realise that a huge sum of money is involved. What is translated here as 'gold coin' was a unit of money known as a 'talent' which was worth over 15 years' wages for a labourer at the time.

The servants that started with 5,000 and 2,000 coins are both congratulated for returning twice that amount to their master. But the servant who hid his master's money, and has done absolutely nothing with it the whole time the master has been away, is condemned.

 # MEDITATIO:

- What does verse 24 reveal about the attitude of the lazy servant to his master?
- What is our attitude to our time and money? Do we consider they belong to us or to God?
- Do we see ourselves as God's servants using our gifts and resources to further God's kingdom on earth?
- What can we learn from the fact that the master gave the servants different amounts according to their ability?

 # ORATIO:

The Psalm for today is a 'wisdom psalm'. It teaches that blessing is to be found in honouring God by living in obedience to him. Pray through these verses from Psalm 128 and ask God to help you to be a good steward of the talents he has entrusted to you.

 # CONTEMPLATIO:

Reflect on all the talents and resources God has given to you. Are you hiding them or are you using them for God's glory?

FAITH IN ACTION

Matthew 25:31-46

[31] "When the Son of Man comes as King and all the angels with him, he will sit on his royal throne, [32] and the people of all the nations will be gathered before him. Then he will divide them into two groups, just as a shepherd separates the sheep from the goats. [33] He will put the righteous people on his right and the others on his left. [34] Then the King will say to the people on his right, 'Come, you that are blessed by my Father! Come and possess the kingdom which has been prepared for you ever since the creation of the world. [35] I was hungry and you fed me, thirsty and you gave me a drink; I was a stranger and you received me in your homes, [36] naked and you clothed me; I was sick and you took care of me, in prison and you visited me.'

[37] "The righteous will then answer him, 'When, Lord, did we ever see you hungry and feed you, or thirsty and give you a drink? [38] When did we ever see you a stranger and welcome you in our homes, or naked and clothe you? [39] When did we ever see you sick or in prison, and visit you?' [40] The King will reply, 'I tell you, whenever you did this for one of the least important of these members of my family, you did it for me!'

[41] "Then he will say to those on his left, 'Away from me, you that are under God's curse! Away to the eternal fire which has been prepared for the Devil and his angels! [42] I was hungry but you would not feed me, thirsty but you would not give me a drink; [43] I was a stranger but you would not welcome me in your homes, naked but you would not clothe me; I was sick and in prison but you would not take care of me.'

[44] "Then they will answer him, 'When, Lord, did we ever see you hungry or thirsty or a stranger or naked or sick or in prison, and would not help you?' [45] The King will reply, 'I tell you, whenever you refused to help one of these least important ones, you refused to help me.' [46] These, then, will be sent off to eternal punishment, but the righteous will go to eternal life."

*Other Readings: Ezekiel 34:11-12, 15-17; Psalm 23:1-3, 5-6;
1 Corinthians 15:20-26, 28*

LECTIO:

This liturgical year draws to a close with the final part of Jesus' fifth discourse in Matthew's gospel. It is not a parable in the strict sense but paints a vivid scene of judgement. It is a complex passage so we will only be able to draw out a few points.

In most of the earlier parables the King represents God the Father. Here Jesus himself is identified as the King who will come to judge all people. Jesus knows that he will be rejected by the religious leaders and crucified. When he returns his true identity will be beyond dispute.

The image of a shepherd separating the sheep from the goats would have been a very familiar one to people in Israel at the time. Sheep and goats grazed together during the day but at night the goats, being less hardy, were separated so they could be kept warm.

The division of the righteous and unrighteous reinforces much of Jesus' earlier teaching. Reaching out in compassion to people around is a natural expression of faith in Jesus. Walking in obedience to Jesus and loving our neighbour leaves no place for being indifferent to the needs of others.

 # MEDITATIO:

- Meditate on Ezekiel 34:11-17. Consider all the different ways the shepherd cares for his sheep. What does this say to you about how God cares for you?
- How does James 2:14-26 help our understanding of this passage?
- How do you respond to the fact that Jesus will come to judge us all?
- What does this passage have to say to us about our attitudes to other people?

 # ORATIO:

Worship Jesus as the King seated on his throne and surrounded by the angels. Ask God to make you responsive to the needs of others. God might speak to you about people who are spiritually, as well as physically, hungry or thirsty.

 # CONTEMPLATIO:

Give thanks that we are reconciled to God because Jesus paid the price for our sin on the cross.

UNITED
BIBLE
SOCIETIES

The United Bible Societies (UBS) is a global fellowship of 145 national Bible Societies operating in over 200 countries and territories. Collectively, the Fellowship is the biggest translator, publisher and distributor of the Bible in the world. Bible Societies are not affiliated to any one Christian Church. They work in partnership with all Christian Churches and many international organisations.

Translating the Bible is at the heart of Bible Society work and our translation policy ensures that we have translation guidelines that are acceptable to the Catholic, Protestant and Orthodox Churches. Bible Societies are also committed to finding new and imaginative ways to draw people into the Bible so that it is central in the material, cultural and spiritual lives of people everywhere. For more details visit: **www.biblesociety.org**

These *lectio divina* outlines are also available in Albanian, Dutch, French, Greek, Maltese, Portuguese, Slovak, Slovenian, Spanish and other languages. For full details visit: **www.wordforliving.org**

For more copies of this book and other resources please contact your national Bible Society.

AUSTRALIA
The Bible Society of Australia
National Scriptures Division
Locked Bag 7003, Minto, NSW 2566
Tel + 61 (02) 9829 9030
www.biblesociety.com.au

CANADA
Canadian Bible Society
10 Carnforth Road, Toronto, Ontario M4A 2S4
Tel 1-416-757-4171
www.biblesociety.ca

IRELAND
The National Bible Society of Ireland
41 Dawson Street, Dublin 2
Tel +353 1 677 3272
www.biblesociety.ie

NAMIBIA
Bible Society of Namibia
Private Bag 13294, #428 Independence Avenue, Windhoek
Tel. +264 (0)61 235 090/1 Fax +264 (0)88 616 726
bsn@nambible.org.na

NEW ZEALAND
The Bible Society in New Zealand
Level 1 Bible House, 144 Tory Street, Wellington 6141
Tel 0800 424253
www.biblesociety.org.nz

SCOTLAND
The Scottish Bible Society
7 Hampton Terrace, Edinburgh EH12 5XU
Tel 0131 347 9813
www.scottishbiblesociety.org

"Your word is a lamp to guide me
and a light for my path."

Psalm 119:105
Good News Bible